## MEMORABLE CLASSES ON MEMORABLE ROUTES

# BULLEID PACIFICS
### on the route from
## WATERLOO
*to*
## WEYMOUTH

Driver Riggs and Fireman Savage of Bournemouth stand beside 'Merchant Navy' Class No 35022 *Holland America Line* at Bournemouth West before departure with a train for Waterloo. *Holland America Line* had entered traffic in October 1948, was rebuilt in 1956, and was withdrawn in May 1966. This very pleasant view epitomises the later years of steam operation on the Waterloo to Bournemouth and Weymouth line. *Ray Ruffell Collection*

# BULLEID PACIFICS

## on the route from

# WATERLOO

### *to*

# WEYMOUTH

## • Chris Harris •

• A SILVER LINK BOOK •

*from*

The NOSTALGIA Collection

First published in 2004

British Library Cataloguing in Publication Data

A catalogue record for this book is available from the British Library.

ISBN 1 85794 232 9

Silver Link Publishing Ltd
The Trundle
Ringstead Road
Great Addington
Kettering
Northants NN14 4BW

Tel/Fax: 01536 330588
email: sales@nostalgiacollection.com
Website: www.nostalgiacollection.com

Printed and bound in Great Britain

# ACKNOWLEDGEMENTS

After well over 30 years in the industry, I think I can say that I am a busman through and through. However, for as long as I can remember I have also been interested in railways, so it was a great privilege to be invited to produce this book about the fascinating Bulleid 'Pacific' locomotives that were so much part of the scene during the latter period of steam operation on the Waterloo to Weymouth line. Writing this book has revived many very happy memories of watching and travelling behind these distinctive locomotives in my younger days.

Peter Townsend of The Nostalgia Collection kindly made available the extensive collection of photographs taken by the late Ray Ruffell, many of which have not previously been published. Brian Jackson from Weymouth has also provided many very interesting photographs, including a number from the late J. D. Blackburn collection. Thanks also to Philip Davies, R. K. Blencowe and Colin Caddy for permission to reproduce photographs. Samantha and Nigel Barnes Evans (The Image Team) from Southampton applied their expertise to produce the map and gradient profile.

Finally I would like to thank Alex Carter, Managing Director, and Andrew Wickham, Operations Director, of Wilts & Dorset Bus Company, for their help and encouragement with this project.

# CONTENTS

Map and gradient profile of the
  Waterloo-Weymouth line                                      6
Table of 'Merchant Navy', 'West Country' and
  'Battle of Britain' 'Pacific' locomotives                    8

Introduction: The man and the machines                       11

Waterloo                                                     15
London to Southampton                                        32
On to Bournemouth, Swanage and Weymouth                      63
The 'Bournemouth Belle'                                     101
Diversionary routes                                         113
Postscript: 'Pacifics' in preservation                     119

Index                                                       128

'West Country' Class No 34020 *Seaton* emerges from the south portal of Bincombe Tunnel running down the 1 in 52 gradient towards Weymouth with the 8.30am service from Waterloo during the summer of 1957. Built as No 21C120 in 1945 and renumbered 34020 in 1948, *Seaton* remained in service until 1964. This locomotive was hauling the 6.30pm Weymouth to Waterloo train on 29 October 1959 when it became derailed at St Denys, and recovery of the locomotive from the sand drag on the approach to the up platform was not completed until a few days later, but fortunately the running lines were not blocked, and trains were able to run normally in the meantime. *The late J. D. Blackburn Collection*

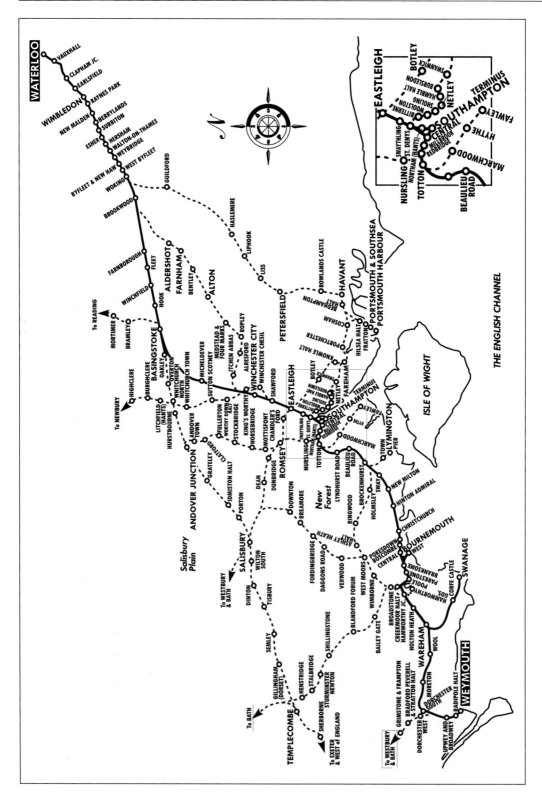

The Waterloo to Weymouth route and surrounding lines in the late 1950s. The map is diagramatic and does not show the complete railway network.

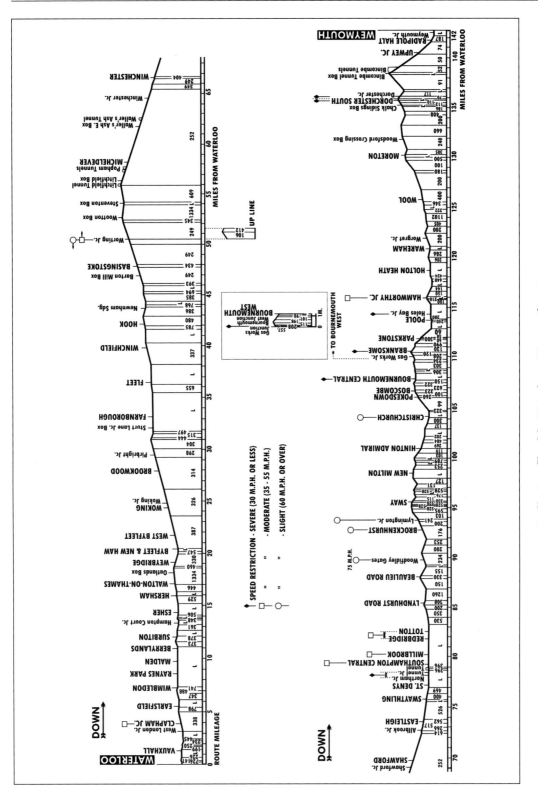

Gradient profile of the Waterloo to Weymouth route.

# Table of 'Merchant Navy', 'West Country' and 'Battle of Britain' 'Pacific' locomotives

## SR 'Merchant Navy' Class 4-6-2

| SR No | BR No | Name | Built | Rebuilt | Withdrawn | |
|-------|-------|------|-------|---------|-----------|---|
| 21C1 | 35001 | *Channel Packet* | 1941 | 1959 | 1964 | |
| 21C2 | 35002 | *Union Castle* | 1941 | 1958 | 1964 | |
| 21C3 | 35003 | *Royal Mail* | 1941 | 1959 | 1967 | |
| 21C4 | 35004 | *Cunard White Star* | 1941 | 1958 | 1965 | |
| 21C5 | 35005 | *Canadian Pacific* | 1941 | 1959 | 1965 | Preserved |
| 21C6 | 35006 | *Peninsular & Oriental S.N. Co* | 1941 | 1959 | 1964 | Preserved |
| 21C7 | 35007 | *Aberdeen Commonwealth* | 1942 | 1958 | 1967 | |
| 21C8 | 35008 | *Orient Line* | 1942 | 1957 | 1967 | |
| 21C9 | 35009 | *Shaw Savill* | 1942 | 1957 | 1964 | Preserved |
| 21C10 | 35010 | *Blue Star* | 1942 | 1957 | 1966 | Preserved |
| 21C11 | 35011 | *General Steam Navigation* | 1944 | 1959 | 1966 | Preserved |
| 21C12 | 35012 | *United States Lines* | 1945 | 1957 | 1967 | |
| 21C13 | 35013 | *Blue Funnel* | 1945 | 1956 | 1967 | |
| 21C14 | 35014 | *Nederland Line* | 1945 | 1956 | 1967 | |
| 21C15 | 35015 | *Rotterdam Lloyd* | 1945 | 1958 | 1964 | |
| 21C16 | 35016 | *Elders Fyffes* | 1945 | 1957 | 1965 | |
| 21C17 | 35017 | *Belgian Marine* | 1945 | 1957 | 1966 | |
| 21C18 | 35018 | *British India Line* | 1945 | 1956 | 1964 | Preserved |
| 21C19 | 35019 | *French Line C.G.T.* | 1945 | 1959 | 1965 | |
| 21C20 | 35020 | *Bibby Line* | 1945 | 1956 | 1965 | |
| | 35021 | *New Zealand Line* | 1948 | 1959 | 1965 | |
| | 35022 | *Holland Amerika Line* | 1948 | 1956 | 1966 | Preserved |
| | 35023 | *Holland Afrika Line* | 1948 | 1957 | 1967 | |
| | 35024 | *East Asiatic Company* | 1948 | 1959 | 1965 | |
| | 35025 | *Brocklebank Line* | 1948 | 1956 | 1964 | Preserved |
| | 35026 | *Lamport & Holt Line* | 1948 | 1957 | 1967 | |
| | 35027 | *Port Line* | 1948 | 1959 | 1966 | Preserved |
| | 35028 | *Clan Line* | 1948 | 1959 | 1967 | Preserved |
| | 35029 | *Ellerman Lines* | 1949 | 1959 | 1966 | Preserved |
| | 35030 | *Elder Dempster Lines* | 1949 | 1958 | 1967 | |

With a rake of Bulleid carriages in tow, the first Bulleid 'Pacific' locomotive, 'Merchant Navy' Class No 35001 *Channel Packet* approaches Bournemouth West with a train from London in the early 1960s. Built in 1941, *Channel Packet* was rebuilt into the form seen here in 1959 and was withdrawn in 1964. *G. Goslin (R. K. Blencowe Collection)*

## SR/BR 'West Country/Battle of Britain' Class 4-6-2

| SR No | BR No | Name | Built | Rebuilt | Withdrawn | |
|-------|-------|------|-------|---------|-----------|---|
| 21C101 | 34001 | Exeter | 1945 | 1957 | 1967 | |
| 21C102 | 34002 | Salisbury | 1945 | | 1967 | |
| 21C103 | 34003 | Plymouth | 1945 | 1957 | 1964 | |
| 21C104 | 34004 | Yeovil | 1945 | 1958 | 1967 | |
| 21C105 | 34005 | Barnstaple | 1945 | 1957 | 1966 | |
| 21C106 | 34006 | Bude | 1945 | | 1967 | |
| 21C107 | 34007 | Wadebridge | 1945 | | 1965 | Preserved |
| 21C108 | 34008 | Padstow | 1945 | 1960 | 1967 | |
| 21C109 | 34009 | Lyme Regis | 1945 | 1961 | 1966 | |
| 21C110 | 34010 | Sidmouth | 1945 | 1959 | 1965 | Preserved |
| 21C111 | 34011 | Tavistock | 1945 | | 1963 | |
| 21C112 | 34012 | Launceston | 1945 | 1958 | 1966 | |
| 21C113 | 34013 | Okehampton | 1945 | 1957 | 1967 | |
| 21C114 | 34014 | Budleigh Salterton | 1945 | 1958 | 1965 | |
| 21C115 | 34015 | Exmouth | 1945 | | 1967 | |
| 21C116 | 34016 | Bodmin | 1945 | 1958 | 1964 | Preserved |
| 21C117 | 34017 | Ilfracombe | 1945 | 1957 | 1966 | |
| 21C118 | 34018 | Axminster | 1945 | 1958 | 1967 | |
| 21C119 | 34019 | Bideford | 1945 | | 1967 | |
| 21C120 | 34020 | Seaton | 1945 | | 1964 | |
| 21C121 | 34021 | Dartmoor | 1946 | 1958 | 1967 | |
| 21C122 | 34022 | Exmoor | 1946 | 1957 | 1965 | |
| 21C123 | 34023 | Blackmore Vale | 1946 | | 1967 | Preserved |
| 21C124 | 34024 | Tamar Valley | 1946 | 1961 | 1967 | |
| 21C125 | 34025 | Whimple | 1946 | 1957 | 1967 | |
| 21C126 | 34026 | Yes Tor | 1946 | 1958 | 1966 | |
| 21C127 | 34027 | Taw Valley | 1946 | 1957 | 1964 | Preserved |
| 21C128 | 34028 | Eddystone | 1946 | 1958 | 1964 | Preserved |
| 21C129 | 34029 | Lundy | 1946 | 1958 | 1964 | |
| 21C130 | 34030 | Watersmeet | 1946 | | 1964 | |
| 21C131 | 34031 | Torrington | 1946 | 1958 | 1965 | |
| 21C132 | 34032 | Camelford | 1946 | 1960 | 1966 | |
| 21C133 | 34033 | Chard | 1946 | | 1965 | |
| 21C134 | 34034 | Honiton | 1946 | 1960 | 1967 | |
| 21C135 | 34035 | Shaftesbury | 1946 | | 1963 | |
| 21C136 | 34036 | Westward Ho! | 1946 | 1960 | 1967 | |
| 21C137 | 34037 | Clovelly | 1946 | 1958 | 1967 | |
| 21C138 | 34038 | Lynton | 1946 | | 1966 | |
| 21C139 | 34039 | Boscastle | 1946 | 1959 | 1965 | Preserved |
| 21C140 | 34040 | Crewkerne | 1946 | 1960 | 1967 | |
| 21C141 | 34041 | Wilton | 1946 | | 1966 | |
| 21C142 | 34042 | Dorchester | 1946 | 1959 | 1966 | |
| 21C143 | 34043 | Combe Martin | 1946 | | 1963 | |
| 21C144 | 34044 | Woolacombe | 1946 | 1960 | 1967 | |
| 21C145 | 34045 | Ottery St Mary | 1946 | 1958 | 1964 | |
| 21C146 | 34046 | Braunton | 1946 | 1959 | 1965 | Preserved |
| 21C147 | 34047 | Callington | 1946 | 1958 | 1967 | |
| 21C148 | 34048 | Crediton | 1946 | 1959 | 1966 | |
| 21C149 | 34049 | Anti-Aircraft Command | 1946 | | 1963 | |
| 21C150 | 34050 | Royal Observer Corps | 1946 | 1958 | 1965 | |
| 21C151 | 34051 | Winston Churchill | 1946 | | 1965 | Preserved |
| 21C152 | 34052 | Lord Dowding | 1946 | 1958 | 1967 | |
| 21C153 | 34053 | Sir Keith Park | 1947 | 1958 | 1965 | Preserved |
| 21C154 | 34054 | Lord Beaverbrook | 1947 | | 1964 | |

| SR No | BR No | Name | Built | Rebuilt | Withdrawn | |
|-------|-------|------|-------|---------|-----------|---|
| 21C155 | 34055 | *Fighter Pilot* | 1947 | | 1963 | |
| 21C156 | 34056 | *Croydon* | 1947 | 1960 | 1967 | |
| 21C157 | 34057 | *Biggin Hill* | 1947 | | 1967 | |
| 21C158 | 34058 | *Sir Frederick Pile* | 1947 | 1960 | 1964 | Preserved |
| 21C159 | 34059 | *Sir Archibald Sinclair* | 1947 | 1960 | 1966 | Preserved |
| 21C160 | 34060 | *25 Squadron* | 1947 | 1960 | 1967 | |
| 21C161 | 34061 | *73 Squadron* | 1947 | | 1964 | |
| 21C162 | 34062 | *17 Squadron* | 1947 | 1959 | 1964 | |
| 21C163 | 34063 | *229 Squadron* | 1947 | | 1965 | |
| 21C164 | 34064 | *Fighter Command* | 1947 | | 1966 | |
| 21C165 | 34065 | *Hurricane* | 1947 | | 1964 | |
| 21C166 | 34066 | *Spitfire* | 1947 | | 1966 | |
| 21C167 | 34067 | *Tangmere* | 1947 | | 1963 | Preserved |
| 21C168 | 34068 | *Kenley* | 1947 | | 1963 | |
| 21C169 | 34069 | *Hawkinge* | 1947 | | 1963 | |
| 21C170 | 34070 | *Manston* | 1947 | | 1964 | Preserved |
| | 34071 | *601 Squadron* | 1948 | 1960 | 1967 | |
| | 34072 | *257 Squadron* | 1948 | | 1964 | Preserved |
| | 34073 | *249 Squadron* | 1948 | | 1964 | Preserved |
| | 34074 | *46 Squadron* | 1948 | | 1963 | |
| | 34075 | *264 Squadron* | 1948 | | 1964 | |
| | 34076 | *41 Squadron* | 1948 | | 1966 | |
| | 34077 | *603 Squadron* | 1948 | 1960 | 1967 | |
| | 34078 | *222 Squadron* | 1948 | | 1964 | |
| | 34079 | *141 Squadron* | 1948 | | 1966 | |
| | 34080 | *74 Squadron* | 1948 | | 1964 | |
| | 34081 | *92 Squadron* | 1948 | | 1964 | Preserved |
| | 34082 | *615 Squadron* | 1948 | 1960 | 1966 | |
| | 34083 | *605 Squadron* | 1948 | | 1964 | |
| | 34084 | *253 Squadron* | 1948 | | 1965 | |
| | 34085 | *501 Squadron* | 1948 | 1960 | 1965 | |
| | 34086 | *219 Squadron* | 1948 | | 1966 | |
| | 34087 | *145 Squadron* | 1948 | 1960 | 1967 | |
| | 34088 | *213 Squadron* | 1948 | 1960 | 1967 | |
| | 34089 | *602 Squadron* | 1948 | 1960 | 1967 | |
| | 34090 | *Sir Eustace Missenden Southern Railway* | 1949 | 1960 | 1967 | |
| | 34091 | *Weymouth* | 1949 | | 1964 | |
| | 34092 | *City of Wells* | 1949 | | 1964 | Preserved |
| | 34093 | *Saunton* | 1949 | 1960 | 1967 | |
| | 34094 | *Mortehoe* | 1949 | | 1964 | |
| | 34095 | *Brentor* | 1949 | 1961 | 1967 | |
| | 34096 | *Trevone* | 1949 | 1961 | 1964 | |
| | 34097 | *Holsworthy* | 1949 | 1961 | 1966 | |
| | 34098 | *Templecombe* | 1949 | 1961 | 1967 | |
| | 34099 | *Lynmouth* | 1949 | | 1964 | |
| | 34100 | *Appledore* | 1949 | 1960 | 1967 | |
| | 34101 | *Hartland* | 1950 | 1960 | 1966 | Preserved |
| | 34102 | *Lapford* | 1950 | | 1967 | |
| | 34103 | *Calstock* | 1950 | | 1965 | |
| | 34104 | *Bere Alston* | 1950 | 1961 | 1967 | |
| | 34105 | *Swanage* | 1950 | | 1964 | Preserved |
| | 34106 | *Lydford* | 1950 | | 1964 | |
| | 34107 | *Blandford Forum* | 1950 | | 1964 | |
| | 34108 | *Wincanton* | 1950 | 1961 | 1967 | |
| | 34109 | *Sir Trafford Leigh-Mallory* | 1950 | 1961 | 1964 | |
| | 34110 | *66 Squadron* | 1951 | | 1963 | |

# INTRODUCTION
# The man and the machines

Oliver Bulleid was born in New Zealand to British parents in 1882, the eldest of three children. In 1889 his father died from pleurisy, and the widowed Mrs Bulleid returned to the United Kingdom with her children. Oliver did well at school, and when he was 18 there were plans for him to return to New Zealand to be articled to a barrister. However, a cousin, Rev Edgar Lee, Vicar of Christ Church, Doncaster, suggested that Oliver should instead train to be an engineer and arranged an interview for him with H. A. Ivatt at that town's Great Northern Railway Works. Commencing his apprenticeship in January 1901, in 1906 Oliver Bulleid was appointed Personal Assistant to the Locomotive Running Superintendent, and progressed to become Assistant to the Locomotive Works Manager a year later.

In March 1908 Bulleid left the Great Northern Railway to take up a position with the Westinghouse Company in France. The increased salary was sufficient for marriage, and he married H. A. Ivatt's youngest daughter in November of that year. After a period living in Europe while working for Westinghouse and for the Board of Trade, Bulleid returned to Doncaster and the Great Northern Railway in 1912 as Assistant to H. N. Gresley. With the Grouping in 1923, Gresley became Chief Engineer of the London & North Eastern Railway, Bulleid becoming his Assistant. In 1937, at the request of Sir Herbert Walker, he applied for the position of Chief Mechanical Engineer of the Southern Railway, succeeding Richard Maunsell.

While he had been working for the LNER Bulleid had been involved with the streamlining of Gresley's 'A4' 'Pacifics', so it is perhaps not too surprising that the 'Pacific' locomotives he designed for the Southern Railway also included streamlining, although in this instance they were described as 'air-smoothed'. The 'Merchant Navy' Class 4-6-2 'Pacifics' began to emerge from Eastleigh Works in 1941. New features included a welded boiler and steel firebox with thermic syphons and a chain-driven motion enclosed in an oil-bath. Four 'Merchant Navy' Class locomotives were completed in 1941, and by 31 July 1942 ten were in service, but it was not until 1 April 1949 that *Elder Dempster Lines*, the last of the 30 'Merchant Navy' Class locomotives, entered traffic.

Meanwhile, in the mid-1940s the Southern Railway Traffic Department needed some lighter main-line locomotives that would have a wider route availability; subsequently, in 1945 the first of no fewer than 110 'Light Pacifics' appeared. Entering service between 1945 and 1951, these 'West Country' and 'Battle of Britain' Class locomotives incorporated the design features of their larger 'Merchant Navy' stablemates, but weighed only 86 tons compared with the almost 95 tons of the latter in working order.

The railways became state-owned from 1 January 1948, the erstwhile Southern Railway forming the Southern Region of the new British Railways. Bulleid retired from the Southern Region on 30 September 1949 and took up the position of Consulting Engineer for Coras Iompair

*Above* Under the skin of a Bulleid 'Pacific': rebuilt 'Merchant Navy' Class No 35029 *Ellerman Lines* is now on display in a sectioned condition at the National Railway Museum, York, as seen here on 7 July 1982. No 35029 entered traffic in February 1949 and was rebuilt in 1959. Transferred to Weymouth in 1964, she was withdrawn in September 1966 and stored at Weymouth shed until April 1967. The National Railway Museum purchased No 35029 from Woodham Brothers of Barry, South Wales, in 1974. *Philip Davies*

*Opposite* 'West Country' Class No 34005 *Barnstaple* entered traffic as No 21C105 in July 1945 and was renumbered in 1948, when the upper photograph was taken at Nine Elms shed. Notice the extended smoke deflectors, fitted for the 1948 locomotive exchanges, in which this locomotive participated. *Barnstaple* was the first of the 'Light Pacifics' to be rebuilt, and the lower photograph shows work in progress at Eastleigh on 22 June 1957. Following rebuilding, *Barnstaple* remained in service until October 1966. *R. K. Blencowe Collection/ E. W. Fry (R. K. Blencowe Collection)*

Eireann at Inchicore, a position he held until his final retirement at the age of 75 in May 1958.

In the mid-1950s the decision was taken by British Railways that the Bulleid 'Pacifics' would be extensively rebuilt. The 'air-smoothed' casing would be removed, the chain-driven motion replaced by Walschaerts valve-gear, a new smokebox fitted, and various other modifications made. The first locomotive to be rebuilt was 'Merchant Navy' Class No 35018 *British India Line*, which re-entered traffic in its modified form in February 1956. Subsequently all 30 of the 'Merchant Navy' locomotives were rebuilt, as were

60 of the 110 'Light Pacifics'; the rebuilding was halted in 1961 when it became clear that the writing was on the wall for steam traction. Although the rebuilding made savings in coal, oil and water consumption and on maintenance, it has to be said that a number of drivers preferred the locomotives in their original form.

After leaving CIE Bulleid retired to Devon, later moving to Malta. He died in April 1970 at the age of 87. In this book we see the magnificent Bulleid 'Pacific' locomotives at work on the Waterloo to Weymouth line, so please join me on a delightful nostalgic journey...

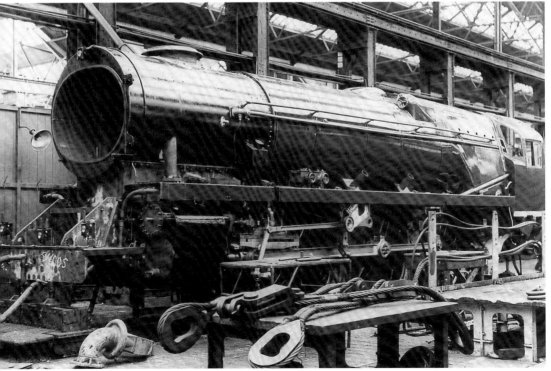

Men and their machines! In the upper photograph we see Bournemouth Driver Joe Langdon on the footplate of 'Merchant Navy' No 35003 *Royal Mail* at Waterloo, after arrival with the up 'Bournemouth Belle' on 19 January 1965. The lower photograph was taken at the other end of the route and shows Driver Bill Smith standing beside 'West Country' No 34010 *Sidmouth* at Weymouth. *Ray Ruffell Collection/the late J. D. Blackburn Collection*

# WATERLOO

Although the first 23 miles of the London &Southampton Railway had opened to the public in May 1838, the original London terminus was situated at Nine Elms. Powers to extend the line further into London, to a terminus in York Road just south of Waterloo Bridge, were obtained in 1845. The new extension left the original line just short of the Nine Elms terminus, and ran mostly on viaduct to the new terminus, which opened on 11 July 1848. There was one intermediate station on the new section of line, at Vauxhall. The original terminus at Nine Elms closed to passengers when the new line opened, but the buildings remained in use as a goods depot until well into the 20th century.

On opening, the 1848 terminus was known as Waterloo Bridge; the present title came into use in 1882. Three additional platforms were added in 1860, while in December 1878 what became known as the 'South Station' was opened, consisting of a long island platform adjacent to, but effectively separate from, the main station. Further expansion came in 1885, when a six-platform station was completed to the north of the 1860 extensions. By 1886 the three sections of the terminus were officially known as Waterloo North, Central and South stations.

Having grown piecemeal over a period of nearly 40 years, Waterloo station was in reality a confused muddle in the late 19th century. The situation was gently lampooned in Jerome K. Jerome's delightful book *Three Men in a Boat*,

published in 1889, but the confusion caused to intending passengers unfamiliar with the bewildering layout was not a joke and the station became the subject of serious press criticism. In 1898 the Board of the London & South Western Railway decided to demolish the entire collection of bits and replace them with a modern purpose-built terminus. A further 6½ acres of land was

**With a Bulleid-designed 4SUB unit in the background, a British Transport Police Inspector keeps an avuncular eye on the comings and goings at Waterloo Station on 1 November 1963.** *Ray Ruffell Collection*

purchased, and site clearance began in 1900; this included the demolition of many houses, whose occupants were relocated into tenement blocks built for them by the LSWR. Work on the new station proceeded in stages through the early years of the 20th century. A significant change from the original plan was the retention of the 1885 North station, which was fully integrated into the new concourse, although the 1885 roof over what became known as the Windsor Line platforms

contributed to a different atmosphere in this part of the station until it was demolished in 1990 to make way for the present Waterloo International.

The completed station was officially opened by HM Queen Mary on 21 March 1922. Built of Portland stone and red brick, Waterloo was transformed into a spacious, convenient and popular station. Moreover, it was to be the last London terminus from which express trains were regularly hauled by steam locomotives.

*Below*  **Where our journey commences: the main pedestrian entrance to Waterloo station is seen on Saturday 6 December 2003. Described as the Victory Arch, this structure was designed by J. R. Scott as a memorial to the 585 London & South Western Railway staff who had lost their lives in the First World War. More irreverently, until glazed doors were fitted at the top of the steps in 1980 this part of the station was known as 'pneumonia corner'! Because the majority of passengers come to Waterloo either by Underground or by taxi relatively few people start their rail journey by walking through this impressive entrance.** *CH*

*Above right*  **On 14 March 1961 rebuilt 'Merchant Navy' Class No 35021** *New Zealand Line* **is seen at the head of the 1.30pm service to Bournemouth. No 35021 entered traffic on 11 September 1948 and was rebuilt in 1959.**

**Withdrawn in 1965, she was later scrapped by Birds at Bridgend, Glamorgan.** *Ray Ruffell Collection*

*Below right*  **The 10.12 excursion to Bournemouth on Sunday 7 May 1961 is formed of Maunsell coaching stock, with 'Merchant Navy' No 35017** *Belgian Marine* **ready to leave Waterloo for the 111-mile run to Bournemouth West. Entering traffic on 17 April 1945 as No 21C17, she was renumbered 35017 in 1948. During the locomotive exchanges of that year she worked between King's Cross and Leeds, and between Euston and Carlisle. No 35017 was rebuilt in 1957 and had run over a million miles when withdrawn in 1966. On the right, 4COR unit No 3108, built in 1937, has arrived with a service from Portsmouth; units of this type remained in traffic until the early 1970s.** *Ray Ruffell Collection*

*Left* At the head of the 3.30pm express to Bournemouth and Weymouth on Thursday 11 May 1961 is 'Merchant Navy' No 35024 *East Asiatic Company*. Entering traffic on 13 November 1948, this locomotive was rebuilt in 1959 and withdrawn in January 1965. Calling at Winchester City, Southampton Central and Brockenhurst, this train will arrive at Bournemouth Central at 5.44pm and divide – the front portion will call at all stations to Weymouth (arrive 7.08pm) while the rear portion, complete with buffet car, will terminate at Bournemouth West at 6.03pm. *Ray Ruffell Collection*

*Below* Having worked an up train from Bournemouth, No 35021 *New Zealand Line* reverses out of Waterloo station on Friday 12 May 1961, making her way to the shed at Nine Elms. Note the former Great Western pannier tank on the right. *Ray Ruffell Collection*

*Right* 'West Country' Class No 34043 *Combe Martin* is ready to depart from Waterloo on 6 July 1961. Built in 1946 as No 21C143, she was renumbered 34043 in 1948 and ran in unrebuilt condition until 1963, when she was withdrawn and subsequently scrapped. Standing alongside is another former GWR pannier tank, No 9770. *Ray Ruffell Collection*

*Below* 'The Royal Wessex' was a titled train introduced to mark the Festival of Britain in 1951, and was the first train on the Bournemouth and Weymouth line to be formed of BR Standard Mark 1 carriages (also newly introduced in 1951). However, on 21 September 1961, as the train leaves Waterloo headed by 'Merchant Navy' Class No 35021 *New Zealand Line*, the first carriage is of Bulleid design. The time is 4.35pm, and 'The Royal Wessex' will arrive at Bournemouth Central at 6.55pm, with the front section continuing to Weymouth (arriving 7.59pm) while the rear of the train (with the restaurant car) will terminate at Bournemouth West at 7.14pm. *Ray Ruffell Collection*

The winter of 1962-3 was exceptionally severe. Christmas 1962 was a very seasonable one, and Boxing Day saw the first snowfalls of the winter in Southern England. On Friday 28 December 1962 we see 'West Country' No 34009 *Lyme Regis* at Waterloo. Built in 1945 as No 21C109, she was renumbered 34009 in 1948, rebuilt in 1961 and withdrawn in 1966. The relatively light snowfall seen here is just a foretaste of what was to come; during the early hours of Sunday 30 December a formidable blizzard blanketed the South of England in deep snow, gale force winds causing considerable drifting. This was followed by a long period during which the daytime temperatures struggled to reach freezing point and the nights were bitterly cold; it was not until early March 1963 that the last of the snow melted. BR Standard 2-6-2 No 82019 is on carriage-shunting duties. *Ray Ruffell Collection*

These two photographs were taken on 22 June 1963 and show No 35030 *Elder Dempster Lines* after arrival at platform 14 with a train from Bournemouth. Rebuilt in 1958, No 35030 had entered traffic on 1 April 1949, the last of the 'Merchant Navy' Class locomotives to do so; it is therefore very appropriate that she worked the last steam-hauled public service train on the Southern Region on Sunday 9 July 1967; this was the 2.07pm from Weymouth to Waterloo, which on that final day of steam arrived at Waterloo a few minutes early. Sadly, after being stored at Nine Elms shed until April 1968, No 35030 was then taken to South Wales and scrapped. *Both Ray Ruffell Collection*

*Above left* The raw winter morning of 30 December 1963 sees a fine line-up of steam locomotives ready to depart with trains from Waterloo. In the right foreground close to the camera is Class 4 4-6-0 No 76065, with a glimpse of 'Merchant Navy' No 35007 *Aberdeen Commonwealth* on the next track behind her. But attention is taken by 'Battle of Britain' Class No 34087 *145 Squadron* seen in the background; built in 1948 and rebuilt in 1960, she was withdrawn in 1967. *Ray Ruffell Collection*

*Left* On Sunday 5 April 1964 'Merchant Navy' No 35011 *General Steam Navigation* reverses out of Waterloo after having worked a train from Bournemouth. This locomotive entered traffic on 30 December 1944 as No 21C11, and was renumbered 35011 in 1948. Rebuilt in 1959, No 35011 was withdrawn in February 1966. In the background, class-mate No 35018 waits to depart with a down service. *Ray Ruffell Collection*

*Top* 'West Country' and 'Battle of Britain' meet at Waterloo on 1 February 1965. On the left No 34103 *Calstock* has charge of the *Canberra* Boat Train to Southampton Docks, which will leave Waterloo at 10.43am. No 34103 was built in 1950 and withdrawn later in 1965. On the right the 10.30am express to Bournemouth and Weymouth is hauled by 'Battle of Britain' No 34089 *602 Squadron*, built in 1948, rebuilt in 1960 and withdrawn in 1967. *Ray Ruffell Collection*

*Above* 'Merchant Navy' Class No 35026 *Lamport & Holt Line* entered traffic on 4 December 1948. Having been rebuilt in 1957, she is seen here reversing out of Waterloo on 12 August 1965 after working an up express from Weymouth. No 35026 was withdrawn in March 1967. *Ray Ruffell Collection*

Boat trains between Waterloo and Southampton Docks were still an important feature of this route during the 1960s. On 3 October 1965 the Greek Line *Arcadia* Boat Train is formed of a mixture of BR Standard Mark 1 and Bulleid stock, and is seen awaiting departure from Waterloo behind rebuilt 'West Country' Class No 34044 *Woolacombe*. Entering traffic as No 21C144 in 1946, this locomotive was renumbered 34044 in 1948, rebuilt in 1960 and withdrawn in 1967. *Ray Ruffell Collection*

A contrast in front ends! 'West Country' No 34093 *Saunton* is emitting copious amounts of steam after arrival with a train from Bournemouth on 13 March 1967. Built in 1949, she was rebuilt in 1960 and withdrawn in 1967. On the right is diesel-electric multiple unit No 1319, one of a number of three-car units built in 1962 for use on the Oxted line. At the time of the photograph No 1319 had just been repainted with all-yellow ends as an experiment, and the unit had been brought to Waterloo for a General Manager's Inspection. The black triangle gave advance warning to platform staff that the guard's section was at that end of the unit. *Ray Ruffell Collection*

No 35013 *Blue Funnel* looks in fine fettle as she reverses out from Waterloo, having worked an up express from Weymouth and Bournemouth on 13 March 1967. This 'Merchant Navy' locomotive entered traffic in February 1945 as No 21C13 and was renumbered 35013 in 1948. She was rebuilt in 1956 and, being based for a while at Exmouth Junction shed, she passed into Western Region stock when the regional boundaries were redrawn from 1 January 1963. Happily she was returned to the Southern, being allocated to Bournemouth in 1964, subsequently passing to Weymouth and finally Nine Elms. The excellent condition of No 35013 in 1967 is borne out in her performance – speeds of well over 100mph were recorded to her credit in April and June of that year. Withdrawn in July 1967, having run more than a million miles, sadly *Blue Funnel* was then scrapped. *Ray Ruffell Collection*

*Right* On Friday 17 March 1967 steam had less than four months left on this line and some workings had already been taken over by diesel traction, but it was still possible to take a photograph at Waterloo that included three steam locomotives and no other forms of traction. Nearest the camera we see the front end of rebuilt 'West Country' Class No 34034 waiting with the 10.43 boat train to Southampton Docks, while 'Merchant Navy' Class No 35007 *Aberdeen Commonwealth* pulls out with the 10.30am express to Weymouth. In the background No 82019 is arriving with a van train from Clapham. *Ray Ruffell Collection*

*Below* A rake of BR Standard Mark 1 carriages has been provided for the 10.30am express to Bournemouth and Weymouth on Sunday 19 March 1967. The leading coach is in the then new blue and grey livery, while the second vehicle is in the more traditional Southern green.

Hauling the train is 'West Country' No 34100 *Appledore*, built in 1949, rebuilt in 1960 and withdrawn in 1967. The Shell Centre and the 1936 signal box make an impressive backdrop. *Ray Ruffell Collection*

Oops! On 28 March 1967 4EPB unit No 5129, working the 9.10am service from Guildford via Cobham, became derailed as it entered platform 3 at Waterloo. Happily nobody was hurt, but the mishap caused considerable disruption for the rest of the day. The disgraced unit is seen on the right of this photograph, which also captures 'West Country' No 34104 *Bere Alston* departing with Bulleid stock on the 10.30am express to Bournemouth and Weymouth. *Bere*

*Alston* was built in 1950, rebuilt in 1961 and withdrawn in 1967. Beside the 10.30am departure is a rake of 4TC stock that has worked an up train from Bournemouth – by this time old and new were working side by side. The 2BIL unit carrying headcode 12 is awaiting departure with a train to Portsmouth & Southsea. *Ray Ruffell Collection*

The 7.05am commuter train from Basingstoke remained steam-hauled until 9 June 1967, and 'West Country' Class No 34024 *Tamar Valley* was allocated for the last steam run, seen here running into Waterloo on that final morning with a mixed rake of Bulleid and BR Standard Mark 1 stock. The same train is seen moments later, after arrival at platform 14 at 8.22am. I wonder how many of the 'city gents' striding purposefully towards the barrier knew (or cared) that this was the last morning that they would be brought to work by steam power. *Tamar Valley* had entered service as No 21C124 in 1946. Renumbered 34024 in 1948 and rebuilt in 1961, she was withdrawn in 1967. *Both Ray Ruffell Collection*

On Wednesday 5 July 1967 the United States Boat Express is hauled by 'West Country' Class No 34025 *Whimple*. Dating from 1946 and numbered 21C125 until 1948, *Whimple* was rebuilt in 1957 and withdrawn in 1967. The Brush Type 4 diesel in the centre is waiting to depart with the 8.30am express to Bournemouth and Weymouth. Six of these diesels were loaned by the Western Region from October 1966 and this timing was one that was often thereafter diagrammed for diesel haulage. Three trains composed of 1937 4COR Portsmouth line stock can be seen, while on the right is a Bulleid-designed 2HAL unit dating from 1939. *Ray Ruffell Collection*

And so to the last day of steam working – Sunday 9 July 1967. At 1.15pm 'West Country' Class No 34021 *Dartmoor* is seen at platform 14 after arrival with the last ever steam-hauled boat train from Southampton Docks. Twenty minutes later (verified by Big Ben!) she reversed out from the terminus for the last time. *Dartmoor* had been built as No 21C121 in 1946; renumbered 34021 in 1948 and rebuilt in 1958, she was now enjoying her final day in service before being taken to Salisbury to be stored before being scrapped. Notice the enthusiasts mourning the demise of steam – this was a sombre day indeed. The honour of working the final steam train into Waterloo on that day fell to 'Merchant Navy' Class No 35030 *Elder Dempster Lines* (see also page 21). *Both Ray Ruffell Collection*

# LONDON TO SOUTHAMPTON

The first section of the London & Southampton Railway, the 23 miles between London and Woking, opened on 21 May 1838, although as we have seen it was not until July 1848 that the present terminus at Waterloo came into use. The extent of the line open to the public was extended over 15 miles west from Woking to Winchfield in September 1838, and the ensuing 7 miles onwards to Basingstoke opened in June 1839.

Construction work had been proceeding at a number of locations between Woking and Southampton, and also opened in June 1839 was the section of line between Southampton and Winchester. Initially the terminus at Southampton

The original terminus of the London & Southampton Railway, opened on 11 May 1840, still stands in 2004, albeit no longer in railway use. On opening the station was called Southampton, being renamed Southampton Docks in 1858 and Southampton Town & Docks in 1896. It was given the name Southampton Terminus in July 1923, and retained this until closure in September 1966. This photograph was taken on Friday 26 March 2004, and shows the handsome building, designed by Sir William Tite, in use as a casino – remarkably little changed in appearance from its days as a station. *CH*

was at Northam, but in May 1840 the line was extended to the station that in due course gained the title Southampton Terminus. During the same month the 18-mile gap between Basingstoke and Winchester was filled, and a special train from London to Southampton ceremonially opened the through route on 11 May 1840.

Proposals to extend the railway westwards from Southampton soon materialised, and the Southampton & Dorchester Railway (see the next chapter) opened in 1847. The original intention was that the Southampton & Dorchester should have a station near the Royal Pier and thence extend to the existing terminal station, but this proposal was vetoed by the harbour authorities. Instead, a 528-yard-long tunnel was built from a station in West Southampton called Blechynden to allow through running for trains from Dorchester to the terminus station. Construction of the tunnel proved difficult, but the line was eventually opened in the summer of 1847.

Any through trains from London to the west of Southampton had to run via the original terminus station and reverse there, but when the London & South Western Railway became responsible for the entire route from London to Dorchester a new spur was opened in August 1858 enabling trains from London to proceed directly to the tunnel and westwards without reversing. This spur required a very sharp curve, which was restricted to 15mph until the 1970s, when some easing of the curvature allowed the speed limit here to be raised to 25mph.

Blechynden station was renamed Southampton West in 1858, but by 1890 the premises were inadequate for the traffic being handled. A replacement station, just west of the original structure, was opened in November 1895. This station was further extended on the down side in the 1930s, and in July 1935 was renamed Southampton Central. Sadly, Southampton Central was badly damaged during the Second World War, a section of the 1930s building being blown to pieces by a parachute mine in June 1941.

The original terminus station had been known simply as Southampton when it opened in 1840. Renamed Southampton Docks in 1858, it became Southampton Terminus in July 1923. By the early 1960s the number of passengers using Southampton Terminus was declining, and an enquiry into the proposal to close the station produced few objections. Southampton Terminus closed to passengers after traffic on Saturday 3 September 1966, but the original 1840 building is listed as being of special architectural and historic interest, and still stands. Today passenger trains from London take the 1858 Northam curve and run through the tunnel to Southampton Central station.

**On 30 December 1963 the 1.15pm boat train from Waterloo to Southampton is formed by an immaculate set of BR Standard Mark 1 carriages hauled by 'Battle of Britain' Class No 34087 145 Squadron, seen here near Vauxhall. Entering service in 1948, No 34087 was rebuilt in 1960 and withdrawn in 1967.** *Ray Ruffell Collection*

On 16 September 1965 the 11.30am service to Bournemouth is also seen passing Vauxhall, and another 'Battle of Britain' locomotive, No 34071 *601 Squadron*, is in charge; that autumn the train was allowed 3 hours to reach Bournemouth Central, with a number of intermediate stops. When No 34071 entered service in 1948 she was the first of the 'Light Pacifics' not to have carried a Southern Railway number in the '21C' series. Rebuilt in 1960, she was withdrawn in 1967.
*Ray Ruffell Collection*

*Right* This view was taken from the front carriage of the 6.23pm empty stock train from Clapham Yard on Friday 30 June 1967, being taken to Waterloo by 2-6-2 tank No 41312, running bunker-first; at the terminus it will form the 6.54pm departure to Basingstoke. Coming towards the camera is the Friday-only 6.22pm relief train from Waterloo to Bournemouth, hauled by 'West Country' Class No 34093 *Saunton*. *Ray Ruffell Collection*

*Below* The 1.30pm express from Waterloo to Bournemouth is formed of Bulleid stock on 22 April 1963, and 'Merchant Navy' No 35023 *Holland Afrika Line* is photographed from the rear cab of the 4SUB unit forming the 1.30pm service from Waterloo to Shepperton. No 35023 entered traffic in November 1948, was rebuilt in 1957 and withdrawn in July 1967. *Ray Ruffell Collection*

*Above* 'Battle of Britain' Class No 34066 *Spitfire* is seen passing Clapham Junction station hauling an up train to Waterloo on 12 June 1965. Entering service in 1947 as 21C166, and renumbered 34066 the following year, *Spitfire* was originally allocated to the Eastern Section of the Southern Region, where she was involved in a serious and remarkable accident at Lewisham. On 4 December 1957 a blanket of dense fog lay across South London, and at around 3.15pm No 34066 left Stewarts Lane Depot for Cannon Street to work the 4.56pm train to Ramsgate. In the thickening fog this journey took much longer than planned and it was not until 4.45pm that No 34066 arrived at Rotherhithe Road Sidings to pick up the carriages; further severe delays resulted in the train finally arriving at Cannon Street station at 5.55pm. For well over an hour the 62-year-old driver waited at the end of the platform in the freezing fog, and when he at last boarded the locomotive he found the water level to be low, with the preparation having been done in anticipation of a 4.56pm start. The driver therefore warned the supervisor at Cannon Street that he would be making an unscheduled stop at Sevenoaks for water.

The train eventually departed at 6.08pm, 72 minutes late and packed with passengers. Following a succession of green signals, the train was travelling at around 30mph at New Cross, but the fog in the ensuing cutting was especially dense. The driver missed the next two signals, which were showing one yellow and two yellows respectively. His fireman looked out at St Johns station, and to his horror saw the signal at danger. 'Red!' he called to his driver, who shut off steam and applied the brakes, but too late; *Spitfire* ran into the rear of the 5.18pm electric train from Charing Cross to

Hayes, which was standing on a rising gradient with its brakes full on. The collision took place below a girder bridge carrying the Nunhead-Lewisham link over the main lines. *Spitfire*'s tender was flung against one of the bridge stanchions, bringing down part of the bridge on to the leading carriages of the train. The locomotive itself was not derailed, but suffered severe front-end damage. Ninety people lost their lives in this tragedy, and more than 170 were injured, many of them seriously. No 34066 was repaired after the accident, and continued in traffic until 1966.

The carriage being shunted on the right is No S3070, a BR Standard Mark 1 Open First built by British Railways' Doncaster Works in 1955. *Ray Ruffell Collection*

*Opposite page* On 7 May 1964 'Merchant Navy' No 35027 *Port Line* is seen in the cutting between Clapham Junction and Earlsfield, heading west with the 1.30pm express from Waterloo to Bournemouth. *Port Line* had entered traffic on 11 December 1948, was rebuilt in 1957 and withdrawn in September 1966. Preserved after withdrawal, in 2004 she resided on the Swanage Railway, but was out of service awaiting repairs to a cracked firebox.

The 1.30pm Waterloo to Bournemouth train is seen again in the lower view, taken on 28 September 1963 near Earlsfield station. 'Merchant Navy' Class No 35021 *New Zealand Line* trails steam as she heads west with a rake of Bulleid carriages built in 1947 for the Bournemouth line – note the extension of the bodyside panelling downwards to cover the solebars, a distinctive feature that much enhanced the appearance of this batch of rolling-stock. *Both Ray Ruffell Collection*

*Above* Back in the 1960s New Year's Day was not a public holiday in England, and 'Merchant Navy' Class No 35007 *Aberdeen Commonwealth* was photographed at Earlsfield heading the 2.54pm service from Waterloo to Basingstoke on the very dull afternoon of 1 January 1964. Entering traffic in June 1942 as 21C7 and renumbered 35007 in 1948, *Aberdeen Commonwealth* was rebuilt in 1958 and withdrawn in July 1967. *Ray Ruffell Collection*

*Below* The rear cab of 4SUB unit No 4741 forming the 1.30pm service from Waterloo to Effingham Junction formed an excellent vantage point from which to photograph 'Merchant Navy' No 35023 *Holland Afrika Line* near Earlsfield with the 1.30pm express from Waterloo to Bournemouth on 21 April 1965. *Ray Ruffell Collection*

*Above* Even in Southern England the weather can spring some surprises. On 21 April 1967 it is just starting to snow as 'West Country' No 34100 *Appledore* nears Wimbledon leading a very mixed rake of coaching stock on the 6.54pm Waterloo to Basingstoke service. *Ray Ruffell Collection*

*Below* From 1962 onwards 'The Royal Wessex' was normally formed of Bulleid rather than BR Standard Mark 1 carriages, and the down train (4.35pm from Waterloo) is seen here between Raynes Park and New Malden on 31 August of that year. Hauling the train is 'Merchant Navy' No 35019 *French Line C.G.T.*, which entered service in June 1945 as 21C19 and was renumbered 35019 in 1948. During that year this locomotive took part in the locomotive exchanges, running between King's Cross and Leeds and between Paddington and Plymouth. Rebuilt in 1959, *French Line C.G.T.* was withdrawn in September 1965. *Ray Ruffell Collection*

For a number of years the Carter's Seeds premises was a landmark beside the line between Raynes Park and New Malden, and part of the building can just be glimpsed on the extreme right of this photograph taken on 29 July 1965. 'Merchant Navy' No 35028 *Clan Line* has charge of the 4.35pm departure from Waterloo – 'The Royal Wessex' – although on this occasion the locomotive is not carrying the familiar headboard. Entering traffic in December 1948, No 35028 was rebuilt in 1959 and withdrawn in July 1967. Immediately on withdrawal *Clan Line* was bought by the Merchant Navy Locomotive Preservation Society, and today still works main-line steam railtours on various routes. *Ray Ruffell Collection*

The signal box at Surbiton seen on the right of the upper photograph came into use on 28 June 1936 and was the first of this distinctive design, later used by the Southern Railway in a number of locations. 'West Country' Class No 34009 *Lyme Regis* is passing at speed with an up train from Bournemouth on 22 April 1964.

Surbiton station was completely rebuilt in 1936-37, the new premises being constructed largely of concrete and including a clock tower of very contemporary design. That tower and part of the footbridge can be seen in the second view, showing another 'West Country' 'Pacific', No 34093 *Saunton*, hurrying towards London with a train from Bournemouth on 8 September 1965. *Both Ray Ruffell Collection*

The Southern Railway rebuilt Woking station during 1936-38, and when this photograph was taken on 10 January 1967 British Rail corporate identity black-on-white platform signage had been installed, although happily the large green and white station nameplates on the ends of the awnings were set to remain for a few more years. 'West Country' Class No 34040 *Crewkerne* is almost enveloped in steam as she passes through with the 1.30pm down express from Waterloo to Bournemouth. Built as No 21C140 in 1946 and renumbered 34040 in 1948, *Crewkerne* was rebuilt in 1960 and withdrawn in 1967. *Ray Ruffell Collection*

On 11 January 1967 the 9.54am from Weymouth (11.07am from Bournemouth) is seen leaving Woking hauled by 'Merchant Navy' No 35014 *Nederland Line*, which at that time was allocated to Weymouth shed. Entering traffic as No 21C14 in February 1945, *Nederland Line* was rebuilt in 1956 and withdrawn in March 1967. *Ray Ruffell Collection*

*Left* On Sunday 15 January 1967 Driver Anderson of Nine Elms and his fireman top up with water at Woking while working the 9.33am Waterloo to Bournemouth excursion. Their locomotive is 'West Country' Class No 34098 *Templecombe* built in 1949, rebuilt in 1961 and withdrawn in 1967. *Ray Ruffell Collection*

*Below left* Without her nameplates, but otherwise looking in fine fettle, 'Battle of Britain' No 34087 *145 Squadron* is seen passing Woking with the 1.30pm express from Waterloo. The top of Woking signal box, opened in 1937, can just be seen above the locomotive tender. *Ray Ruffell Collection*

*This page* Ancient and Modern at Woking – motive power, not hymn books! The electrification in 1967 extended the third rail as far west as Branksome, with passenger trains being powered by diesel locomotives between Bournemouth and Weymouth. To avoid passengers having to change trains at Bournemouth, a push-and-pull system was developed whereby a high-powered four-car electric multiple unit (4REP) normally formed the London end of the train with one or two unpowered four-car multiple units (4TC) at the 'country' end. One or both of the 4TCs were taken between Bournemouth and Weymouth by a push-pull-fitted diesel-electric locomotive of the D65XX series. On 3 March 1967 the first of the 4REP units, No 3001, is seen on test at Woking beside 'Battle of Britain' No 34060 *25 Squadron* on an up train from Bournemouth. When first introduced, the new electric stock was painted in an overall blue livery that looked very dull; repainting in Inter-city blue and grey was soon ordered!

The second photograph was taken through the driving cab window of the 4REP unit as No 34060 pulled out of the station; I think the looks on the faces of the steam locomotive crew say it all! *Both Ray Ruffell Collection*

*Above* When deliveries of the 4REP electric multiple units commenced, the 10.30am service from Waterloo became an electric train between Waterloo and Bournemouth, running to the steam timings, from Monday 3 April 1967. The leading 4TC unit was then taken on from Bournemouth to Weymouth by a D65XX diesel-electric locomotive. This photograph shows 'Merchant Navy' No 35030 *Elder Dempster Lines* passing through Woking with this train on Friday 31 March 1967 – the last weekday it was planned for steam haulage. *Ray Ruffell Collection*

*Below* Bereft of her nameplates and smokebox door numberplate, 'Merchant Navy' Class No 35013 *Blue Funnel* trundles through Woking with the 11.05am parcels train from Waterloo to Basingstoke on 12 May 1967 – a very menial task for this magnificent locomotive. No 35013 was still capable of much better things, and the following month was recorded travelling at no less than 106mph with a passenger train. *Ray Ruffell Collection*

Ray Ruffell took these photographs from a vantage point beside the line between Sturt Lane and Farnborough during the morning of Sunday 12 September 1965. 'West Country' Class No 34040 *Crewkerne*, built in 1946, rebuilt in 1960 and withdrawn in 1967, is seen on the down line with the 9.22am Waterloo to Bournemouth excursion, while 'Battle of Britain' No 34088 *213 Squadron* approaches with an up boat train from Southampton. The latter locomotive was built in 1948, rebuilt in 1960 and withdrawn in 1967. *Both Ray Ruffell Collection*

On Sunday 2 July 1967 British Rail ran two special 'Farewell to Steam' excursions from Waterloo. The first left the terminus at 9.55am hauled by 'Merchant Navy' Class No 35008 *Orient Line* and ran through to Weymouth. The return departure from the Dorset resort was at 3.00pm and the up train was photographed near Farnborough as *Orient Line* powers towards London.

The second train was a round trip from Waterloo to Bournemouth, departing Waterloo at 12.20pm. It was in the care of another 'Merchant Navy' 'Pacific', No 35028 *Clan Line*, and the return journey gets a friendly wave from a lineside observer near Farnborough. *Both Ray Ruffell Collection*

The 7.08am commuter train from Basingstoke to Waterloo has just departed from Farnborough on the morning of 7 July 1964. Hauling this ten-coach train is 'West Country' No 34046 *Braunton*, built in 1946, rebuilt in 1959 and withdrawn in 1965. *Braunton* has been preserved, and at the time of writing is in the care of the West Somerset Railway. *Ray Ruffell Collection*

*Above* 'West Country' Class No 34102 *Lapford* stands at the end of the down platform at Farnborough station on Monday 18 September 1961. *Lapford* entered service in 1950 and was withdrawn in 1967. Note the signal box and signal gantry; the 23 miles of route between Woking and Basingstoke was equipped with a pneumatic signalling system in 1904, which remained in use until 1966. *Ray Ruffell Collection*

*Below* First stop Basingstoke! The 5.30pm Waterloo to Bournemouth train thunders through Farnborough on 13 April 1964 with 'West Country' No 34046 *Braunton* in charge. This train was allowed 1 minute under 3 hours to travel the 111 miles from Waterloo to Bournemouth West, with 11 intermediate stops. *Ray Ruffell Collection*

By the late spring of 1967 Farnborough station had new platform lighting and British Rail corporate identity signs. London-bound commuters wait in their usual positions along the platform on 9 May 1967 as their train, the 7.05am Basingstoke to Waterloo, pulls in behind 'West Country' Class No 34047 *Callington*. Built in 1946 as 21C147, *Callington* was renumbered 34047 in 1948, rebuilt in 1958 and withdrawn in 1967.

Steam had exactly one month left on this particular service, and sister locomotive No 34024 *Tamar Valley* is seen in the lower view performing the final honours on Friday 9 June (see also page 29 for arrival at Waterloo). From Monday 12 June 1967 this became an electric service, working initially to the steam timings. *Both Ray Ruffell Collection*

*Right* 4REP unit No 3001 was on test with a 4TC unit on the four-track section between Basingstoke and Woking on 3 March 1967, and the upper photograph was taken through the rear cab window of the latter when the train was travelling at 80mph. 'Battle of Britain' No 34088 *213 Squadron*, built in 1948 and rebuilt in 1960, is rapidly overtaking with an up express from Bournemouth – obviously still capable of a fine performance despite impending withdrawal. *Ray Ruffell Collection*

*Below* Westwards from Basingstoke the line continues as four tracks for 2¾ miles to Worting Junction, where the line to Salisbury and Exeter diverges from the line to Southampton and Weymouth. 'West Country' Class No 34102 *Lapford* was photographed heading westwards 'light engine' along this four-track section on Wednesday 5 July 1967. *Both Ray Ruffell Collection*

A period of just under three years separates these two photographs taken at the west end of Basingstoke station. In the upper photograph, taken on 12 July 1964, 'Merchant Navy' No 35016 *Elders Fyffes* is seen passing through at speed with a down express for Bournemouth and Weymouth consisting mainly of BR Standard Mark 1 stock.

The lower photograph was taken on 16 May 1967 and shows 'West Country' No 34102 *Lapford* after arrival at Basingstoke with the 5.39pm commuter train from Waterloo. This train has quite a mixed rake of stock; the leading vehicle is a BR Standard Mark 1 First in British Rail blue and grey, followed by a Bulleid-designed Second in Southern green. It is the third carriage that is of

particular interest: it is an early BR Standard Mark 2 side-corridor First, one of a batch of 20 built for the Southern Region in 1964. These vehicles, delivered in Southern green, were part of the very first production batch of Mark 2 carriages, and were destined to remain the only examples on the Southern Region for a number of years. It is an irony that electrification would return those First Class travellers who had enjoyed the appointments of this carriage to travelling in Mark 1 stock! *Lapford* has attracted some admirers on the platform, for steam has little time left – the conductor rails are in place and energised, and it will be noticed that the semaphore signals seen on the gantry in the 1964 view have been replaced by colour lights. *Both Ray Ruffell Collection*

*Above* From September 1962 the 'Pines Express' through service from Manchester to Bournemouth was re-routed away from the Somerset & Dorset line, running instead via Reading and joining the Waterloo to Weymouth line at Basingstoke. 'West Country' Class No 34040 *Crewkerne* is seen approaching Eastleigh with the Bournemouth-bound 'Pines' on 30 April 1965. The train left Manchester (Piccadilly) at 10.00am, and *Crewkerne* would have taken over at Oxford at 2.04pm; arrival at Bournemouth West was scheduled for 4.44pm. The train is formed of BR Standard Mark 1 carriages in maroon livery. *Ray Ruffell Collection*

*Below* On 10 July 1965 'Merchant Navy' No 35028 *Clan Line* roars over the points at 80mph on the down fast line at Eastleigh with the 10.30am express from Waterloo to Bournemouth and Weymouth. The line to Chandlers Ford and Romsey can be seen curving away in the left background; the regular passenger service along that route was withdrawn in May 1969, but over the years a number of through passenger trains have continued to use the line, and eventually Chandlers Ford station was re-opened, with a regular service to Southampton, in 2003. *Ray Ruffell Collection*

**Below** Relief trains were a regular feature of the 1960s railway scene. On 10 July 1965 'Battle of Britain' No 34064 *Fighter Command* passes through Eastleigh

station on the down fast line with a relief express from Waterloo to Bournemouth. Entering service in 1947 as 21C164, *Fighter Command* was renumbered 34064 in 1948 and survived in unrebuilt condition until withdrawal in 1966. However, a very significant modification was made to this locomotive in 1962 when a Giesl oblong ejector was fitted in place of the conventional chimney. This gave better steaming and also reduced the emission of sparks, and the narrow oblong chimney can just be discerned in this photograph. Standing at platforms 1 and 3 of Eastleigh station are three-car 'Hampshire' diesel-electric multiple units dating from 1957; units of this type took over many local services in Hampshire from the late 1950s onwards. *Ray Ruffell Collection*

**Below** On the same day sister locomotive No 34076 *41 Squadron* approaches Eastleigh with an up express from Bournemouth to Waterloo. *41 Squadron* was built in 1948 and withdrawn in 1966. No doubt the fireman is anticipating the next 15 miles up to Litchfield, nearly all on a gradient of 1 in 252 against the locomotive in this direction. The large Southern Railway notice seen at the platform end in the left foreground prohibits railway employees from taking a short cut to the works or depot by walking along the track. *Ray Ruffell Collection*

On the afternoon of 13 March 1966 the 4.45pm van train to Clapham is seen at Eastleigh Carriage Sidings – an easy task for 'Merchant Navy' No 35017 *Belgian Marine*. Although still carrying her nameplates, *Belgian Marine* has lost the number plate from her smokebox door, so in place of it somebody has chalked '21C17', the Southern Railway number given in April 1945. When this photograph was taken *Belgian Marine* had only a few more weeks left in service, being withdrawn in July. *Ray Ruffell Collection*

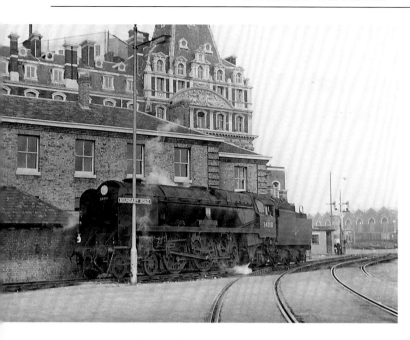

*Left* When photographed on 16 October 1960, 'West Country' Class No 34018 *Axminster*, running 'light engine', had just crossed Canute Road at the east end of Southampton Terminus station and entered the Eastern (Old) Docks. *Axminster* entered service as 21C118 in 1945, was renumbered 34018 in 1948, rebuilt in 1958 and withdrawn in 1967. *R. K. Blencowe Collection*

*Below* Another 'West Country', No 34093 *Saunton*, is seen here at Southampton Old Docks with the empty stock from a boat express on 5 February 1964. *Ray Ruffell Collection*

Above 'West Country' Class No 34097 *Holsworthy* had worked the Northern Star Boat Train from Waterloo when this photograph was taken at Southampton Old Docks on 20 July 1965. *Holsworthy* entered service in 1949, was rebuilt in 1961 and withdrawn in 1966. The tank engine on the left, No 30067, was built at the Vulcan Iron Works of Wilkes-Barre, Pennsylvania, USA, in 1943 and was one of a batch of 14 0-6-0 United States Transportation Corps shunting locomotives acquired by the Southern Railway in 1945. *Ray Ruffell Collection*

Below On 19 August 1965 'West Country' No 34033 *Chard* is seen arriving at Southampton Ocean Terminal in the Eastern Docks past a choice selection of 1960s cars. *Chard* had entered service as 21C133 in 1946, was renumbered 34033 after nationalisation, and was withdrawn in 1965. *Ray Ruffell Collection*

The afternoon of Sunday 1 July 1962 saw two non-stop trains to Waterloo depart from platform 1 at Southampton Central within 10 minutes of each other. In the upper photograph 'West Country' No 34017 *Ilfracombe* has arrived with the 3.15pm express from Bournemouth West to Waterloo, and is awaiting the departure time of 4.05pm with a mixed rake of Maunsell and Bulleid carriages. Numbered 21C117 when entering service in 1945, *Ilfracombe* became 34017 in the British Railways era, was rebuilt in 1957 and withdrawn in 1960.

After the departure of this train, 'Merchant Navy' No 35027 *Port Line* arrived at 4.11pm with the 2.20pm service from Weymouth to Waterloo; the fireman can be seen topping up with water prior to departure at 4.15pm. *Both Ray Ruffell Collection*

'Merchant Navy' No 35017 *Belgian Marine* has charge of the 1.00pm Bournemouth West to Waterloo semi-fast service on 31 March 1964. In the first photograph the train can be seen pulling away from platform 1 at Southampton Central, then the camera has been turned through 180 degrees to record the scene as the locomotive passes the photographer and heads for Southampton Tunnel. Having departed Southampton Central at 2.15pm, this train will now call at Eastleigh, Winchester City, Basingstoke and Woking before arrival at Waterloo at 4.09pm. The office block that dominates the background of the lower view was built on the site of the old Grand Theatre, which had been demolished after closure in 1959; the classical-styled building just to the right of this is Southampton Bus Station, opened in 1933 and closed in 1987, the site now being occupied by part of the Marlands Shopping Centre. *Both Ray Ruffell Collection*

Driver Hawkins of Nine Elms is about to depart westwards from Southampton Central with the 11.30am service from Waterloo on 13 March 1966. His locomotive is 'West Country' No 34038 *Lynton*, built as 21C138 in 1946, renumbered 34038 by British Railways and withdrawn in June 1966. The leading carriage is a side corridor Second, also of Bulleid design. *Ray Ruffell Collection*

# ON TO BOURNEMOUTH, SWANAGE AND WEYMOUTH

A single-track railway between Blechynden station in Southampton (see previous chapter) and Dorchester was opened in 1847. The chief promoter of this line was a Wimborne solicitor, Charles Castleman, who had devised a route via Brockenhurst, Ringwood, Wimborne and Wareham, thus linking as many towns as possible, albeit at the cost of a rather circuitous end-to-end route – the line soon came to be known as 'Castleman's Corkscrew'! Bournemouth, then a small village with a population of around 200, was not served, but a branch line from Hamworthy Junction ran to a station in Lower Hamworthy that was given the name Poole.

The line from Southampton to Dorchester was doubled between 1857 and 1863, and a branch line from Brockenhurst to Lymington was opened in 1858. In November 1862 a branch line opened between Ringwood and Christchurch; this was extended to Bournemouth in 1870, the terminal station later becoming known as Bournemouth East.

In 1872 a line opened that left 'Castleman's Corkscrew' at Broadstone and ran to Poole, with a station much more conveniently located for the

This platform was all that remained in 2004 of the original Southampton & Dorchester Railway station for Poole. Opened on 1 June 1847, the station was renamed Hamworthy when a new station for Poole was opened in 1872 virtually on the site of the present Poole station (see also page 87). The original station was closed to passengers on 1 July 1896, but a freight line from Hamworthy Junction remains, as seen in this photograph, taken on Friday 26 March 2004. *CH*

Opened in 1874 and considerably enlarged in 1888, Bournemouth West was the terminus for trains from the Somerset & Dorset Line, from Salisbury and from Brockenhurst via West Moors (the 'old road'), as well as for the Bournemouth portions of trains from London Waterloo. This photograph was taken on 29 August 1965; sadly this popular station, which seemed to have had a special atmosphere of its own, was closed the following month. The buildings were demolished in 1970, and a coach park now occupies the site. *Ray Ruffell Collection*

town; this line was extended to a terminus at Bournemouth West in 1874. A line connecting Bournemouth East and Bournemouth West opened in 1888, as did a direct line between Brockenhurst and Christchurch – finally giving the by now rapidly expanding town of Bournemouth a direct rail link with London.

In 1893 a direct link was opened between Poole and Hamworthy Junction via a causeway across Holes Bay, but the passenger service between Hamworthy and the original Poole station in Lower Hamworthy was discontinued in 1896.

The opening of the direct route from Brockenhurst had reduced the Ringwood-Christchurch branch to a quiet backwater, which eventually closed in 1935. The line from Brockenhurst via Ringwood and Wimborne to Hamworthy, known to generations of local railwaymen from 1888 onwards as the 'old road', remained a useful diversionary route, but was closed to passengers in May 1964.

Bournemouth West station closed to passengers in 1965, although the viaduct that once carried the sharply curved link from Gasworks Junction still stood in 2004, albeit devoid of track. As part of the 1967 electrification a new depot was established on the former approach tracks to Bournemouth West, but trains from the east access this by reversal in Branksome station. Bournemouth West station was demolished in 1970.

A branch line from Wareham via Corfe Castle to Swanage opened in May 1885, and can be included within the scope of this book because it enjoyed through services to and from Waterloo that were often hauled by a Bulleid 'West Country' or 'Battle of Britain' 'Pacifics' on summer Saturdays during the 1950s and 1960s. Some through services to Waterloo continued after 1967, provided by 4TC units powered by a D65XX locomotive between Swanage and Bournemouth, but through services between Swanage and London were discontinued in October 1969 and the Swanage branch was closed to passengers in January 1972. However, that was not the end of the story, as we shall see in the final chapter...

Meanwhile, in 1847 the western terminus of 'Castleman's Corkscrew' in Dorchester had been built on an east-west alignment with the intention that the line would in due course continue westwards to Exeter. In the event this did not happen, and a link was made with the Great Western Railway route from Yeovil to Weymouth, which opened in 1857. This resulted in the LSWR station at Dorchester acquiring a curious layout whereby down trains from London to Weymouth called at a through platform, while up trains from Weymouth to London had to run past the station and reverse into the original terminus platform. This arrangement persisted until a new up platform was provided on the curve opposite the down platform in 1970. Dorchester South station was completely rebuilt in 1986.

From Dorchester to Weymouth, trains from Waterloo had running powers over the Great Western line opened in 1857, the tracks being of dual gauge to allow the running of the LSWR trains before the GWR converted the line from broad to standard gauge in 1874. Weymouth station was built by the GWR, and had an overall roof; this was largely dismantled in 1951, leaving some rather strangely shaped platform canopies. In 1950 the Southern Region was given full responsibility for the route beyond Dorchester, the regional boundary being moved to Sparkford on the former GWR Weymouth-Westbury line. The station at Weymouth received a coat of Southern Region green and cream paint, and an additional island platform was added in 1957; this now forms the nucleus of the present Weymouth station, which was rebuilt in 1986 to occupy a much smaller area. Electrification was extended from Bournemouth to Weymouth in 1988.

**During the last week of steam operation on the Waterloo-Weymouth line, on Friday 7 July 1967, the 11.25am service from Weymouth to Waterloo approaches Southampton from Millbrook, headed by** **'Merchant Navy' Class No 35008 *Orient Line*. Built as 21C8 in 1942, *Orient Line* was renumbered 35008 by British Railways in 1949, rebuilt in 1957 and withdrawn in 1967.** *Ray Ruffell Collection*

On the previous day, Thursday 6 July 1967, 'Battle of Britain' Class No 34087 *145 Squadron* passes the photographer with the same train. Again, these pictures illustrate the mix of carriage types that had become a feature of this route during the last years of steam, in contrast to the set formations of a few years earlier. It will be noted that the front carriage of the train is the same on both days – S4324S, a Bulleid-designed semi-open Brake Second built at Eastleigh in 1947. Note the Ford Anglia car parked on Saxon Road on the right – one of the most popular cars of the mid 1960s. *Both Ray Ruffell Collection*

The London & South Western Railway purchased the Southampton Dock Company in 1892, and illustrations in the previous chapter show trains on lines in the Old (or Eastern) Docks that were laid by the railway company towards the end of the 19th century. By the 1920s there was a demand for additional dock capacity at Southampton, and work began to reclaim an area of 400 acres of mudlands near Millbrook, which came into use as Southampton New Docks in the 1930s; the rail connection via Millbrook to the New Docks opened in June 1935. 'West Country' No 34102 *Lapford* is seen after arrival at the New Docks with the *Oriana* Boat Train on 17 May 1963.

The second photograph is of great interest, illustrating a little-known working. On occasions special bullion trains were operated between Southampton Docks and London, and for obvious reasons these movements were not publicised. This photograph was taken on Monday 3 July 1967 and shows the last steam-hauled bullion special making its way along the line between Millbrook and Southampton Central. The locomotive is 'West Country' No 34036 *Westward Ho!* built in 1946, rebuilt in 1960 and withdrawn in 1967. *Both Ray Ruffell Collection*

Brand spanking new! 'Merchant Navy' Class No 35024 is seen attached to a 'Battle of Britain' tender with an up train at Boscombe station on 27 November 1948. As yet un-named, the locomotive is painted in matt malachite green, and carries the wording 'British Railways' on the tender. Subsequently, on 5 May 1949, No 35024 was named *East Asiatic Company* at Waterloo station by HRH Prince Axel of Denmark, Chairman of that company. Rebuilt in 1959, *East Asiatic Company* was withdrawn in January 1965, having run a total of 839,415 miles. Boscombe station was opened in June 1897 in response to local requests; sadly this spacious and elegant station was closed in October 1965. *Brian Jackson*

*Above* 'Merchant Navy' Class No 35025 was only eight weeks old when photographed working the 11.12am service to Waterloo on 25 January 1949. No 35025 had entered traffic on 27 November 1948 and would be given the name *Brocklebank Line* by Colonel Bates, Chairman of that shipping company, at Waterloo on 20 September 1949. *Brocklebank Line* was rebuilt in 1956, and fortunately was preserved after withdrawal in 1964. *R. K. Blencowe Collection*

*Below* With the blower on to draw the fire, 'Merchant Navy' Class No 35027 waits to depart from Bournemouth Central with an up train in June 1949. Painted in malachite green, the nameplates are boarded over prior to the locomotive being named *Port Line* by that company's Chairman, Mr W. Donald, in a ceremony at Southampton Docks on 24 April 1950. *Brian Jackson*

'West Country' Class No 34005 *Barnstaple* stands on the up through line at Bournemouth Central as sister locomotive No 34008 *Padstow* departs with an up express. *Barnstaple* was built as 21C105 in July 1945, and renumbered 34005 in June 1949. Subsequently rebuilt in 1957, it was withdrawn in October 1966. *Padstow* was built in September 1945 as 21C108 and renumbered 34008 in April 1949. Rebuilt in 1960, *Padstow* was withdrawn in June 1967. *Brian Jackson*

Named after the wartime General Manager of the Southern Railway, 'Battle of Britain' Class No 34090 *Sir Eustace Missenden Southern Railway* departs from Bournemouth Central with an up express during the 1950s. Built in February 1949, No 34090 was subsequently rebuilt in 1960 and withdrawn at the end of Southern Region steam operation in July 1967, having run 743,948 miles. *Brian Jackson*

Two further portraits of locomotives at Bournemouth feature, first, 'Battle of Britain' Class No 34084 *253 Squadron* preparing to depart from Central with a train for Waterloo on 28 November 1960; the leading carriage is of Maunsell origin. New in 1948, No 34084 remained in unrebuilt form until taken out of service in 1965.

In the second photograph we see that the leading carriage of the Waterloo express headed by 'West Country' No 34021 *Dartmoor* on Saturday 24 June 1961 is also a Maunsell vehicle, although the next carriage is a modern BR Standard Mark 1 Brake Second. The signals are off, but No 34021's tender water tank is still being topped up prior to departure. *R. K. Blencowe Collection/Ray Ruffell Collection*

On 18 August 1962 'West Country' No 34016 *Bodmin* emerges from the bridge under Holdenhurst Road to enter the down platform at Bournemouth Central. Entering service as 21C116 in November 1945, *Bodmin* was renumbered 34016 in 1948, rebuilt in 1958 and withdrawn in June 1964. Preserved after withdrawal, *Bodmin* now resides on the Watercress Line in Hampshire (see also page 120). Notice the trolleybus wires along Holdenhurst Road, just visible above the bridge parapet in the background. Bournemouth Corporation Service 25, which ran along Holdenhurst Road, was converted to motor-bus operation in September 1965, but trolleybuses continued in use in Bournemouth until April 1969. *Ray Ruffell Collection*

Having worked in with a service from Weymouth on 18 August 1962, 'Merchant Navy' No 35008 *Orient Line* reverses down one of the two non-platform lines that ran through Bournemouth Central Station. These tracks were removed at the time of electrification in 1967, but their former presence accounts for the unusually large gap between the two through platforms that still exists at this station. *Ray Ruffell Collection*

A magnificent photograph of the very first of the Bulleid 'Pacifics'. 'Merchant Navy' Class No 35001 *Channel Packet* heads an up express for Waterloo at Bournemouth Central on 22 June 1964. Named at Eastleigh Works by the Minister of Transport, Rt Hon J. T. C. Moore Brabazon on 10 March 1941, and entering traffic in June of that year as 21C1, *Channel Packet* was subsequently renumbered 35001 in 1949. Rebuilt in 1959, she had only a few months left in service when this photograph was taken, being withdrawn in November 1964.

*Ray Ruffell Collection*

The rationalised track layout at Bournemouth Central station in 1967 is only too apparent in this photograph of 'Merchant Navy' No 35003 *Royal Mail* at the head of the Locomotive Club of Great Britain's 'Dorset Coast Express' railtour; the centre lines have gone and the conductor rail is in place ready for electric services. Having entered service on 13 September 1941 as 21C3, this locomotive was named *Royal Mail* by Lord Essendon, Chairman of Royal Mail Lines, at Waterloo station in October of that year, and subsequently renumbered 35003 in 1948. Rebuilt in 1959, No 35003 remained in service until the end of steam on the Waterloo-Weymouth line in July 1967. *Ray Ruffell Collection*

In steam days Bournemouth locomotive depot was situated at the west (Weymouth) end of Bournemouth Central station; in 2004 the site is occupied by a car park. 'West Country' No 34012 *Launceston* was photographed at Bournemouth shed in June 1954; she entered traffic as 21C112 in October 1945 and was renumbered in 1948. Subsequently rebuilt ten years later, *Launceston* was taken out of service in 1966.

In the lower view 'Merchant Navy' No 35010 *Blue Star* sports a large 'crease' in her 'air-smoothed' casing as she shunts around at Bournemouth, probably in 1956. Built in 1942 as 21C10 and renumbered 35010 in 1948, *Blue Star* was rebuilt in 1957 and withdrawn in September 1966. *R. K. Blencowe Collection/Brian Jackson*

*Opposite page* A familiar piece of railway equipment in steam days that has been made completely obsolete by conversion to electric or diesel working is the turntable. 'West Country' Class No 34104 *Bere Alston* is seen on the turntable at Bournemouth shed on 1 July 1962, while sister locomotive No 34094 *Mortehoe* is seen at the shed a few weeks later on 18 August. Entering traffic in October 1949, No 34094 was withdrawn from service in August 1964. *R. K. Blencowe Collection/Ray Ruffell Collection*

*Above* 'Cab of a Powerhouse': a close-up view of 'Merchant Navy' No 35020 *Bibby Line* laying over at Bournemouth shed on 18 August 1962. Entering traffic as No 21C20 in June 1945, this locomotive was named *Bibby Line* by the Chairman of the shipping company, Mr H. Bibby, at Waterloo on 18 October that year. *Bibby Line* was involved in an incident at Crewkerne while working the 2.25pm Plymouth to Waterloo service on 24 April 1953. Approaching the station at around 80mph, the locomotive's middle driving axle fractured, and brake gear hurled from the locomotive as a result hit the cast-iron supports of the up platform canopy with such force that they snapped, bringing down a section of the canopy. In the aftermath of this incident all of the 'Merchant Navy' locomotives were temporarily withdrawn for a short period in May 1953 while their axles were examined and tested. Train services were maintained by locomotives loaned by other regions, which even resulted in Eastern Region 'V2s' working expresses between Waterloo and Bournemouth! *Bibby Line* was back in service in July 1953 and was rebuilt in 1956. Withdrawn in February 1965, No 35020 was subsequently cut up at Eastleigh Works, the only member of the class to be scrapped at the same location as it was built. *Ray Ruffell Collection*

On Sunday 12 March 1961 'Battle of Britain' No 34057 *Biggin Hill* leaves platform 4 at Bournemouth West with a rake of Bulleid and Maunsell carriages forming the 2.15pm express to Waterloo. Calling at Bournemouth Central, Brockenhurst and Southampton Central, this train is due to terminate in London at 4.44pm. *Biggin Hill* entered traffic in March 1947 as 21C157 and was renumbered 34057 in 1949. Withdrawal came in May 1967, a few weeks before the end of steam on the Southern Region. Notice the 'Hampshire' diesel-electric multiple unit just visible in platform 3 on the right.

The lower photograph was taken on the same day, and shows 'West Country' No 34095 *Brentor* at Bournemouth West, waiting to work a train to Waterloo. Built in 1949, *Brentor* was rebuilt in 1961 and withdrawn in 1967. *Both Ray Ruffell Collection*

'Battle of Britain' No 34088 *213 Squadron* looks in fine fettle at the head of a gleaming rake of Bulleid stock on the 2.15pm express to Waterloo on 25 February 1962. Driver Dick Thomas of Nine Elms looks out from the cab as he awaits departure time from Bournemouth West.

In the lower photograph Driver Weatherley and his fireman are on platform 2 of Bournemouth West station, beside 'West Country' No 34006 *Bude*. Entering traffic as 21C106 in July 1945, *Bude* was renumbered 34006 in 1948 and withdrawn in March 1967. *Both Ray Ruffell Collection*

*Above* Journey's end! On 29 August 1965 'West Country' Class No 34046 *Braunton* has just arrived at platform 5 at Bournemouth West with the 9.30am service from Waterloo, consisting of a rake of BR Standard Mark 1 stock. This was the main arrival platform for trains for Waterloo, with the majority of the London departures leaving from platform 4. *Ray Ruffell Collection*

*Below* When the previous photograph was taken, the closure of Bournemouth West to passengers was imminent; that accounts for the complete lack of people in this view, which provides a fine overall view of the station area on 13

October 1965. For a while after closure to passengers some services continued to run as empty stock between Bournemouth West and Bournemouth Central, and we see 'Battle of Britain' No 34079 *141 Squadron* leaving platform 4 with the stock for the 3.09pm service from Bournemouth Central to Waterloo. No 34079 had entered service in July 1948 and was withdrawn in February 1966. Bournemouth West's six platform faces, which were numbered from platform 1 on the right of this view, can be clearly seen. Platforms 4, 5 and 6 were longer than 1, 2 and 3, and the main station buildings were beside platform 4. The station was finally demolished in 1970. *Ray Ruffell Collection*

Parkstone station is situated on a short 1 in 300 section part way up the formidable 1 in 60 Parkstone bank. Trains climb the bank in the up direction, and in this view we see the 'Bournemouth Belle' (see also the next chapter) headed by 'Battle of Britain' No 34061 *73 Squadron* passing through the station. On this occasion the 'Belle' had been diverted via Ringwood, so was approaching Bournemouth from the west rather than from the east. Built as 21C161 in April 1947 and renumbered 34061 in 1949, *73 Squadron* was withdrawn in 1964. *R. K. Blencowe Collection*

The 1872 station at Poole had sharply curving platforms at which, until 1961, all passenger trains were required to stop. 'West Country' No 34102 *Lapford* is seen on an up service, formed of Bulleid stock, while another train, also formed of Bulleid carriages, occupies the down platform. Poole station was extensively rebuilt in 1969-70 in preparation for the construction of the Towngate flyover, and was again rebuilt in 1988. *M. Wyatt (R. K. Blencowe Collection)*

The final Bulleid 'Pacific' locomotive to be built was 'Battle of Britain' Class No 34110 *66 Squadron*, which was completed in January 1951. In this photograph, taken at Wareham on 24 March of that year, No 34100 is seen when still in 'showroom condition' with a rake of Bulleid carriages. *66 Squadron* was taken out of service in November 1963. *R. K. Blencowe Collection*

The single-track branch for Swanage left the main Waterloo-Weymouth line at Worgret Junction, a short distance west of Wareham station. Through services to and from Waterloo often brought 'West Country' and 'Battle of Britain' 'Pacifics' on to the Swanage branch during the 1950s and 1960s, and here an up train from Swanage to Waterloo, hauled by 'West Country' No 34106 *Lydford*, is seen approaching the main line at the junction. *Lydford* entered service in 1950 and was withdrawn in September 1964. The train is formed of 'ironclad' carriages dating from the early 1920s. *R. K. Blencowe Collection*

Local trains between Swanage and Wareham were normally operated by three-car 'Hampshire' diesel-electric multiple units from 5 September 1966 onwards. However, until July 1967 a number of steam-hauled special trains continued to visit the branch at weekends. On Sunday 7 May 1967 the Locomotive Club of Great Britain ran the 'Dorset Coast Express' railtour, which was headed by 'West Country' Class No 34023 *Blackmoor Vale*. Built in February 1946 as 21C123 and renumbered 34023 in 1948, *Blackmoor Vale* is seen by the buffer stops at Swanage station; note the Bell & Cronin train departure board just visible on the left. The second photograph shows the same train at Corfe Castle.

The Swanage branch was closed to passengers in January 1972, but has been re-opened between Swanage and Norden by preservationists as the Swanage Railway (see page 124). *Blackmoor Vale* was preserved after withdrawal in July 1967, and now resides on the Bluebell Railway in East Sussex, where the nostalgic can enjoy the delightful experience of travelling in a Bulleid or Maunsell (or even earlier) carriage hauled by a 'West Country' locomotive (see pages 119 and 123). *Both Ray Ruffell Collection*

The original station at Dorchester opened in 1847 as a terminus on an east-west alignment, it being intended that the line would eventually be extended to Exeter. Instead a link with the Great Western Railway route from Yeovil to Weymouth was opened in 1857. This eventually resulted in a very unusual layout here: down trains from Waterloo to Weymouth had a normal through platform, brought into use in 1879 and visible in the left foreground of the upper photograph, on the curve to the GWR, while up trains from Weymouth to Waterloo continued past the station, then reversed into the (original) up platform. These photographs, dating from 1956 and showing 'West Country' No 34006 *Bude* heading a Weymouth to Waterloo service, illustrate the procedure. It was not until 1970 that a new up platform was finally provided opposite the down platform on the curve to eliminate this reversing movement, and even then the buildings on the old up platform remained in use, linked to the new up platform by a walkway, until the station was completely rebuilt in 1986. *Both Colin Caddy Collection*

Upwey & Broadwey station was opened in April 1886 as a junction station for the Abbotsbury branch, which had opened in November 1885. Situated about 440 yards south of the former Upwey station that it replaced, the new facility was called Upwey Junction until the Abbotsbury branch was closed in 1952. On 18 September 1959 'Merchant Navy' No 35001 *Channel Packet* passes through with the 5.35pm Weymouth to Waterloo service. The former Abbotsbury branch platform is immediately behind the vegetation on the right of the photograph.

The lower view shows 'West Country' No 34001 *Exeter*

approaching Upwey & Broadwey station on the climb out of Weymouth. *Exeter* was built as 21C101 in 1945, renumbered 34001 in 1949, rebuilt in 1957 and withdrawn in July 1967. The pointwork under the locomotive leads to the former Abbotsbury branch; after closure, a short spur remained open for goods until January 1962. In its day the Abbotsbury branch had been a delightful operation, with an auto-train meandering through the countryside searching for passengers – the kind of line that inspired the wonderful film comedy *The Titfield Thunderbolt*. *Both the late J. D. Blackburn Collection*

On 29 April 1959 Her Majesty the Queen, accompanied by Prince Charles, travelled to Weymouth and Portland. The Royal Train, hauled by 'West Country' Class No 34048 *Crediton*, is first seen passing Weymouth engine sheds on the approach to Weymouth station, where the Royal party alighted. *Crediton* was built as 21C148 in 1946, renumbered 34048 in 1948, rebuilt in March 1959 and withdrawn in March 1966.

Having visited HMS *Eagle*, the Royal party rejoined the train at Portland Dockyard, the special being hauled over the branch by former GWR pannier tank locomotives Nos 3737 and 4624. Onwards from Weymouth Junction the train was double-headed by 'West Country' locomotives Nos 34048 *Crediton* and 34046 *Braunton*; the lower photograph shows the train climbing away from Weymouth towards Radipole Halt, heading for Windsor. Note the well-wishers on the embankment on the right.
*Both the late J. D. Blackburn Collection*

Nearly there! 'Battle of Britain' No 34060 25 Squadron approaches Weymouth station with a mixed rake of Bulleid and BR Standard Mark 1 carriages. Built in 1947 as 21C160, 25 Squadron was renumbered 34060 in 1948, rebuilt in 1960 and withdrawn in July 1967. M. Wyatt (R. K. Blencowe Collection)

Weymouth shed was originally built by the Great Western Railway, and was situated beside the down line about three-quarters of a mile north of Weymouth station. The turntable seen in the upper photograph, occupied by 'West Country' No 34031 *Torrington* on 20 August 1960, was installed in 1925. *Torrington* entered service as 21C131 in June 1946, was renumbered 34031 in 1949, rebuilt in 1958 and withdrawn in February 1965. The lower photograph shows 'Merchant Navy' Class No 35013 *Blue Funnel* at Weymouth shed in 1964.
*Both R. K. Blencowe Collection*

Two newly rebuilt locomotives are seen at Weymouth shed. The first photograph shows 'Merchant Navy' No 35016 *Elders Fyffes* on the turntable during the summer of 1957. Built as 21C16 in 1945, *Elders Fyffes* was renumbered 35016 in 1948, rebuilt in 1957 and withdrawn in 1965. In the lower photograph 'West Country' No 34048 *Crediton* stands outside the shed after working the Royal Train to Weymouth on 29 April 1959 (see page 93).*Crediton* had been rebuilt the previous month. *Both the late J. D. Blackburn Collection*

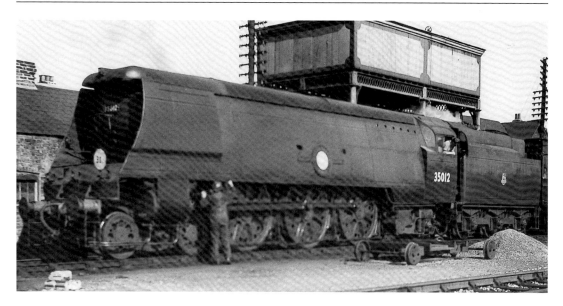

Before and after: in the first photograph 'Merchant Navy' No 35012 *United States Line* stands in the old engine siding at Weymouth station during the early 1950s. Notice the GWR water tank in the background; prior to 1885 the original GWR locomotive shed had stood in the area to the left of the locomotive in this photograph. *United States Line* had entered traffic as 21C12 in January 1945, was renumbered 35012 in 1949 and was subsequently rebuilt in 1957. The lower photograph was taken on 16 November 1960 and shows the rebuilt locomotive approaching Weymouth Junction with a special train consisting of five First Class Pullman carriages, *Juno*, *Alicante*, *Daphne*, *Cassandra* and *Niobe*, conveying guests who were to be wined and dined aboard the new cross-Channel steamer *Caesarea* as she cruised in the English Channel. From Weymouth Junction the special was taken along the harbour tramway to Weymouth Quay station by former GWR 0-6-0PT No 1367. *Both the late J. D. Blackburn Collection*

*Above* New 'West Country' locomotive No 34091 is officially named at Weymouth station on 29 December 1949 by the Mayor of Weymouth and Melcombe Regis, Alderman Alfred Percy Burt. No 34091 remained in service until 1964. *The late J. D. Blackburn Collection*

*Below* 'Battle of Britain' No 34110 *66 Squadron* arrives at Weymouth with the down 'Royal Wessex' one evening during the summer of 1951. *66 Squadron* was the last Bulleid 'Pacific' locomotive to be built, and entered service in January 1951. The train consists of BR Standard Mark 1 stock, also built in 1951 – very appropriate for a new service introduced that year to celebrate the Festival of Britain. *66 Squadron* was withdrawn in December 1963, having run a recorded 609,147 miles. *The late J. D. Blackburn Collection*

Driver Hutton of Bournemouth and his fireman are ready to depart from platform 3 at Weymouth with the 3.50pm service to Waterloo on 3 February 1965. Their locomotive is 'Battle of Britain' No 34086 *219 Squadron*, which entered traffic in December 1948 and was withdrawn in June 1966. Notice the ornate gas lamps on the platform. In the background the 1957 signal box is just visible; this remained in use for 30 years, being closed in 1987. *Ray Ruffell Collection*

The end of the line, 142¾ miles from Waterloo: the buffer stops at Weymouth station. This photograph shows 'West Country' Class No 34023 *Blackmoor Vale* at the 'country' (or should that be 'seaside'?) end of platform 3 after arrival with the Locomotive Club of Great Britain's 'Dorset Coast Express' railtour on Sunday 7 May 1967. Although the station building has acquired a British Rail corporate identity sign, the paintwork is still Southern Region green and cream. *Blackmoor Vale* has attracted quite a crowd of admirers! *Ray Ruffell Collection*

# THE 'BOURNEMOUTH BELLE'

The all-Pullman 'Bournemouth Belle' was introduced in 1931; the inaugural train on 5 July that year was headed by 'King Arthur' Class No E780 *Sir Persant*. Initially timed to leave Waterloo at 10.30am, on weekdays the train divided at Bournemouth Central with the front portion proceeding to Weymouth while the remainder of the train continued to Bournemouth West; on Sundays the entire train terminated at Bournemouth West.

The 'Bournemouth Belle' ran on Sundays throughout the year, but when the weekday service was re-introduced with the 1932 summer timetable Weymouth was no longer served, the

**'Merchant Navy' No 35018 *British India Line* gets the heavy all-Pullman 'Bournemouth Belle' under way from Waterloo at 12.30pm on Sunday 8 October 1961. Entering traffic as 21C18 in May 1945, this locomotive had the distinction of hauling the first post-war 'Bournemouth Belle' on 7 November 1946, and was renumbered 35018 in 1948. *British India Line* was the first of the Bulleid 'Pacifics' to be rebuilt, the work being carried out at Eastleigh between November 1955 and February 1956. Withdrawn in August 1964, No 30518 is now preserved – see page 125.** *Ray Ruffell Collection*

entire train terminating at Bournemouth West on all days of operation until the closure of that station in 1965, when Bournemouth Central became the terminus. The pattern of running on weekdays during the summer season and all year round on Sundays continued until 1 January 1936, when the 'Bournemouth Belle' became a daily service throughout the year.

Suspended during the Second World War, the 'Bournemouth Belle' was re-instated on 7 November 1946 when the familiar 12.30pm departure time from Waterloo was established. At first the return journey left Bournemouth West at 7.15pm, but from the start of the 1947 summer timetable this was brought forward to 4.35pm.

Bulleid 'Pacific' locomotives were normally used on the 'Bournemouth Belle' from 1946 onwards, although the Southern Region diesel-electric locomotives Nos 10201 and 10202 were also used in the early 1950s. Regular steam haulage of the 'Bournemouth Belle' was planned to cease from 2 January 1967, with the duty being given to one of the Brush Type 4 diesels on loan from the Western Region. However, right up to the last week of steam operation on the line, Bulleid 'Pacifics' were sometimes substituted for the diesels on the 'Bournemouth Belle'. On Monday 3 July 1967 'West Country' Class No 34025 *Whimple* worked the train in both directions, while on Wednesday 5 July the down train was powered by 'West Country' No 34024 *Tamar Valley*, while sister locomotive No 34036 *Westward Ho!* was provided for the up working. *Westward Ho!* therefore had the distinction of hauling the very last steam-worked 'Bournemouth Belle'.

Sadly there was no place for an all-Pullman train after the line was electrified, and the 'Bournemouth Belle' ran for the last time, hauled both ways by Brush diesel No D1924, on Sunday 9 July 1967.

*Left* On 26 March 1964 'Merchant Navy' No 35008 *Orient Line* is making good progress through the sinuous curves out of Waterloo station, running beside a 4SUB unit – also designed by Oliver Bulleid and dating from the late 1940s. *Ray Ruffell Collection*

*Above* On 1 May 1966 Brush Type 4 diesel-electric No D1686, on loan from the Western Region, was turned out for the down 'Bournemouth Belle'; the train is seen leaving Waterloo in front of the 1936 signal box. *Ray Ruffell Collection*

*Below* Four months earlier, on 4 January, a steam locomotive, No 35008 again, had been provided for this duty, when the 11-coach train was photographed passing Clapham Junction 'A' signal box. On 10 May the previous year corrosion in the supporting girders had caused this structure to partly collapse during the height of the morning peak period, with the result that all trains to and from Waterloo had to be turned short (in some cases as far out as Surbiton or Woking) for the rest of the day. Immediate steps having been taken to support the signal box, full main-line services were restored from the following day. *Ray Ruffell Collection*

'Merchant Navy' No 35005 *Canadian Pacific* takes water during the stop at Southampton Central with the down 'Bournemouth Belle' on 31 March 1964. *Canadian Pacific* entered traffic in January 1942 as 21C5, and was renumbered 35005 in 1948. Rebuilt in 1959, she was withdrawn in October 1965, and after some years at Barry, South Wales, was eventually preserved. *Ray Ruffell Collection*

Driver Ray Foyle of Bournemouth was working the down 'Bournemouth Belle' with 'Merchant Navy' Class No 35003 *Royal Mail* on 19 January 1965 when these photographs were taken at Southampton Central. What a pity that the headboard was often not used by the mid-1960s. *Both Ray Ruffell Collection*

The sharp curve between the spur from Bournemouth West and the main Weymouth-Waterloo line at Gas Works Junction is well illustrated in these photographs. In the first 'Merchant Navy' No 35014 *Nederland Line* enters the curve at Bournemouth West Junction with the up 'Bournemouth Belle', while the lower view looks along the rake of Pullman cars forming the up service on 29 August 1965 as the train passes over the Bourne Valley viaduct; 'West Country' No 34037 *Clovelly* provided the motive power on that day (see also page 110). *R. K. Blencowe Collection/Ray Ruffell Collection*

On 8 April 1962 'Merchant Navy' No 35029 *Ellerman Lines* is nearing journey's end at Bournemouth West with the down 'Bournemouth Belle'. In the right foreground 'West Country' No 34006 *Bude* waits in platform 2 prior to working the 3.15pm service from Bournemouth West to Waterloo. *Ray Ruffell Collection*

'Merchant Navy' Class No 21C11 *General Steam Navigation*, built in 1944, is seen in July 1948 in Southern Railway malachite green livery just a few months after nationalisation waiting to leave platform 4 at Bournemouth West with the up 'Bournemouth Belle'. Renumbered 35011 in November, *General Steam Navigation* was rebuilt in 1959 and withdrawn in 1966. Compare the headboard in use here with that seen in the 1961 photograph on page 101. *R. K. Blencowe Collection*

These photographs were taken on 21 June 1964 and show 'Merchant Navy' No 35026 *Lamport & Holt Line* at Bournemouth West with the up 'Bournemouth Belle'.

The driver is Jack Pett of Nine Elms; his fireman is fortifying himself with a mug of tea before the serious coal shovelling that lies ahead! *Both Ray Ruffell Collection*

Although the 'Bournemouth Belle' was normally worked by the larger 'Merchant Navy' locomotives, sometimes a 'Light Pacific' was used. Such was the case on 29 August 1965 when 'West Country' No 34037 *Clovelly* was photographed at Bournemouth West. Built as 21C137 in August 1946, *Clovelly* was renumbered 34037 in 1949, rebuilt in 1958 and withdrawn in July 1967. A week after this photograph was taken the 'Bournemouth Belle' was truncated to run between Waterloo and Bournemouth Central only; less than two years later the train was withdrawn altogether, having no place in the new electric era... *Ray Ruffell Collection*

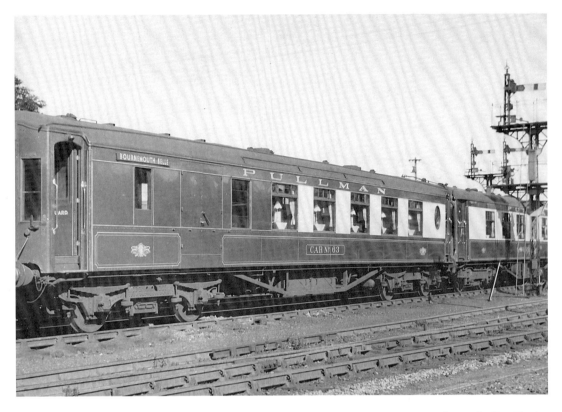

Of course most passengers using the 'Bournemouth Belle' were more interested in the luxurious appointments of the Pullman cars, many of which were quite elderly by the 1960s. The cars illustrated in these photographs were from a batch built by the Midland Carriage & Wagon Company in 1928. Car No 63, photographed at Bournemouth West on 9 September 1962, is a Brake Second, while Car No 61, photographed at Clapham on 13 March 1967, is a Kitchen Second. *Both Ray Ruffell Collection*

Kitchen Car No 167 was built by the Midland Carriage & Wagon Company in 1924, and is seen at Bournemouth West on 10 March 1963.

A few modern cars were cascaded on to the 'Bournemouth Belle' during the train's last years of operation, and one such was First Class Kitchen Car *Orion*, built in 1951 by the Birmingham Carriage & Wagon Company for the 'Golden Arrow' service between London Victoria and Dover, but on 13 March 1967 seen in the 'Bournemouth Belle' formation at Clapham. *Orion* has been preserved by Pecorama at Beer in Devon, where it is still possible in 2004 to enjoy afternoon tea in this (albeit static) car. *Both Ray Ruffell Collection*

# DIVERSIONARY ROUTES

Travel by rail at weekends, especially on Sundays, is sometimes affected by engineering work that can often result in trains being diverted by unusual routes.

The electrification works for the route from Waterloo to Bournemouth included re-ballasting and relaying the track between Brookwood and Branksome with continuous welded rail.

Schedules were decelerated from the autumn of 1965 to make some allowance for the inevitable delays that this work would cause, and at weekends there were many instances of Bulleid 'Pacific' locomotives hauling Waterloo-Weymouth services being diverted away from the normal line.

A few examples of diverted trains during the 1960s are recorded in this chapter.

It was cold and freezing hard on Sunday 8 December 1963 when the 9.33am Waterloo to Bournemouth excursion was diverted via Alton and then 'over the Alps' via Alresford to Winchester. The train, headed by 'West Country' No 34009 *Lyme Regis*, consisted of 13 carriages, so Type 3 diesel-electric No D6532 was attached at Alton to provided assistance up the severe climb to Medstead. The combination of steam and diesel is seen here about to leave Alton station. The line between Alton and Winchester was closed by British Rail in February 1973, but the section between Alton and Alresford has been re-opened by preservationists as the Mid Hants Railway (see page 120).
*Ray Ruffell Collection*

Close to London, services are sometimes diverted between Woking and Clapham Junction by leaving the main line at Byfleet and running via Staines and Feltham. This route was also, in fact, followed by the steam trains that operated between Poole and Waterloo on 9 July 2003 and between Wareham and Waterloo on 6 December 2003 (see pages 126 and 127).

These photographs were taken on 28 November 1965, when engineering works made such a diversion necessary. In the first view 'Merchant Navy' No 35013 *Blue Funnel* is passing through Egham station on the 8.53am service from Bournemouth to Waterloo, while in the lower view 'Battle of Britain' No 34088 *213 Squadron* is leaving a fine trail of steam with the 8.20am Weymouth to Waterloo service between Egham and Staines. *Both Ray Ruffell Collection*

Another route often used by diverted trains during the electrification works on the Bournemouth line was the Portsmouth line via Guildford to Havant, then continuing via Fareham to Southampton. On 13 March 1966 the 11.30am Waterloo to Weymouth service was so diverted, and 'West Country' No 34038 *Lynton* is seen being topped up with water at Guildford station.

'Battle of Britain' No 34051 *Winston Churchill* was photographed laying over at Guildford on 13 July 1965. This locomotive entered service as No 21C151 in December 1946, and was renumbered 34051 in 1948. Sir

Winston Churchill died on 24 January 1965, and following a state funeral at St Paul's Cathedral on Saturday 30 January, his body was taken by a special train from Waterloo station to Handborough on the Western Region – the nearest station to his burial place at Bladon, near Blenheim Palace. Appropriately this train was hauled by 'Battle of Britain' Class No 34051 *Winston Churchill*. Withdrawn by British Rail in September 1965, this locomotive has subsequently been preserved as part of the National Railway Museum Collection. *Both Ray Ruffell Collection*

We can follow the diverted progress of 'West Country' No 34038 *Lynton* on the 11.30am Waterloo to Weymouth service on 13 March 1966, which we first encountered at Guildford on the previous page. Having travelled via Petersfield and Havant, the train leaves the Waterloo to Portsmouth line at Farlington Junction and is about to pass rebuilt sister locomotive No 34040 *Crewkerne* heading the similarly diverted 9.54am Weymouth to Waterloo service.

Between Woolston and Bitterne the railway follows the shoreline of the River Itchen, which is tidal at this point; it is clearly low tide as *Lynton* passes. The train will rejoin the main line at St Denys. *Both Ray Ruffell Collection*

Slightly away from our featured route, but very close to the diversionary route illustrated on the previous two pages, 'West Country' Class No 34103 *Calstock* is seen on pilot duties at Portsmouth & Southsea (Low Level) on 7 July 1965. This locomotive has only a few weeks left in service, being withdrawn in September of that year. Beyond *Calstock* is three-car 'Hampshire' diesel-electric multiple unit No 1111. This type of unit provided the majority of services on the Portsmouth-Southampton-Salisbury line between 1957 and 1990. In 1979-80 this particular unit was to undergo an experimental refurbishment at Eastleigh, becoming Second Class only and gaining improved lighting and luggage racks. No 1111 retained these features until withdrawal, but was the only unit in the series to be so treated. Just arriving at platform 3 on the right is 2BIL electric unit No 2063 forming the 9.27am service from Waterloo; these units were associated with the semi-fast and stopping services between Waterloo and Portsmouth from 1937 until around 1970. *Ray Ruffell Collection*

Prior to its closure in May 1964, the 'old road' via Ringwood was used as a diversionary route (see also page 86). 'Battle of Britain' No 34060 *25 Squadron* is seen during the 1950s at Holmsley, running light. *25 Squadron* was subsequently rebuilt in 1960 and withdrawn in 1967.

After closure to passengers, Ringwood station remained open for freight, served from the Broadstone direction, until August 1967. On 21 May 1966 'West Country' No 34006 *Bude* visited with the 'Hampshire Explorer' railtour and is seen facing the New Street level crossing; the unusual footbridge will be noted. Ringwood station has subsequently been demolished and a road, called Castleman Way, now runs where the train is standing in the photograph. *Both R. K. Blencowe Collection*

# POSTSCRIPT: 'PACIFICS' IN PRESERVATION

The introduction of the full electric service between Waterloo and Bournemouth from 10 July 1967 spelled the end for steam operation on the Waterloo to Weymouth route.

We are, however, most fortunate that no fewer than 11 'Merchant Navy' Class and 20 'West Country'/'Battle of Britain' Class locomotives have been preserved. Thus it is still possible to enjoy Bulleid 'Pacific' haulage on some of the delightful 'heritage' railways, while in recent years there have even been instances of some of these magnificent locomotives being used to haul special trains on main lines – including the Waterloo to Weymouth route.

I particularly enjoy visiting the Bluebell Railway in East Sussex, where it is sometimes possible to travel in a Bulleid or Maunsell carriage behind a Bulleid 'Pacific' locomotive. Being the first standard gauge passenger line to be taken over by enthusiasts, the Bluebell had the opportunity to take into stock a substantial collection of pre-nationalisation carriages as they were withdrawn from revenue-earning service, and this, in my opinion, adds considerably to the authenticity of the experience (see also page 123).

'West Country' No 21C123 *Blackmoor Vale* was photographed during a visit on Monday 30 July 2001. Seen here immaculately restored in Southern Railway malachite green livery, *Blackmoor Vale* was built in 1946, given the BR number 34023 in 1948, and for a long time carried nameplates spelled *Blackmore Vale*. Withdrawal from BR service came with the end of steam on the Waterloo to Weymouth line in July 1967, but in the ownership of the Bulleid Society Ltd the locomotive continues to delight visitors to the Bluebell Railway. *CH*

On page 113 we saw how the route via Alton and Alresford to Winchester was sometimes used as a diversionary route when the main Waterloo to Weymouth line was unavailable because of engineering work. The line between Alton and Winchester was closed by BR in February 1973, but the section between Alton and Alresford has been re-opened by preservationists as the Mid Hants Railway. Because of the steep gradients this line was known to railwaymen as 'going over the Alps'; the route is also known as the 'Watercress Line' from its former role of carrying this

Hampshire produce to the London markets. Preserved 'West Country' No 34105 *Swanage* was photographed at Alton on 20 September 1987, working tender-first with a rake of BR Standard Mark 1 stock. *Swanage* was built in 1950 and withdrawn from BR service in 1964.

In the photograph of the locomotive yard at Ropley, taken on 22 January 1990, 'West Country' No 34016 *Bodmin* stands in the foreground, with *Swanage* just visible behind 'M7' 0-4-4T No 245, which dates from 1897 and is now part of the National Railway Museum Collection. *Both Ray Ruffell Collection*

*Above* Another 'West Country' locomotive that has been preserved is No 34092 *City of Wells*, at the time of writing resident on the Keighley & Worth Valley Railway in West Yorkshire. Built in 1949 and withdrawn by British Railways in 1964, *City of Wells* is seen in Woking station yard on 29 May 1988, taking part in the 'Woking 150' event that commemorated the opening of the railway to Woking in 1838. *Ray Ruffell Collection*

*Below* 'West Country' Class No 34027 *Taw Valley* was built in 1946, rebuilt in 1957 and withdrawn by British Railways in 1964. Now privately owned, in 2004 *Taw Valley* was located at the Severn Valley Railway in Worcestershire. She is seen here on 19 February 1994 at Waterloo, posed next to diesel-electric multiple unit No 205028, operating 'The Thumper Tribute' railtour. *Both Ray Ruffell Collection*

Saturday 18 May 2002 saw preserved 'Merchant Navy' No 35005 *Canadian Pacific* with 'The Dorset Coast Express' railtour at Weymouth station. Unlike the railtours that had carried that title in 1967 (see pages 78 and 90), the 2002 train had started from Alton and had run to Weymouth via Woking, Salisbury, Yeovil and Maiden Newton; the train was hauled from Yeovil to Weymouth by a diesel locomotive, *Canadian Pacific* following tender-first. Re-attached to the train at Weymouth station, this magnificent locomotive is seen prior to departure on the return leg of the railtour, which ran via the main Weymouth-Waterloo line to Woking. *Both Philip Davies*

It wasn't just the locomotives... It is probably apparent that I also had a soft spot for the distinctive Bulleid carriages that were still to be found in quantity on the Waterloo to Bournemouth and Weymouth line right until the end of steam operation in 1967, long after pre-nationalisation carriages had been ousted by BR Standard types on most other main lines. We are indeed fortunate that some of this comfortable stock survives in preservation. These photographs were taken on the Bluebell Railway in Sussex in July 2001, and show exterior and interior views of a 64-seat Open Third (later Second) built at Eastleigh in 1950. The lozenge-shaped toplights in the doors are a quick recognition feature for Bulleid carriages. Note the very appropriate Waterloo-Weymouth roofboard! *Both CH*

Closed by British Rail in January 1972, the Swanage branch has since been re-opened by preservationists between Swanage and Norden (just on the Wareham side of Corfe Castle). During the afternoon of Good Friday, 9 April 2004, 'West Country' Class No 34028 *Eddystone* is seen ready to depart from Swanage station with a train for Norden. *Eddystone* had been built as 21C128 in 1946 and was renumbered 34028 in 1948. Rebuilt in 1958, in 1964 she was the first rebuilt Bulleid 'Light Pacific' to be withdrawn by British Rail. Forty years later *Eddystone* is seen in gleaming condition, having recently re-entered service after expert attention in the Swanage Railway's Herston Works.

'Battle of Britain' No 34072 *257 Squadron* entered traffic in April 1948. Although the squadron after which the locomotive was named flew from the airfield we now know as Bournemouth International Airport, No 34072 was initially based at Dover, later moving to Exmouth Junction and finally to Eastleigh not long before withdrawal in October 1964. In preservation *257 Squadron* was active on the Swanage Railway for more than 12 years before being withdrawn in 2003, her boiler certificate having expired. There are plans to overhaul her and return her to traffic on the Swanage Railway, and on Friday 9 April 2004 she was parked in Swanage station, with the public invited to visit her footplate. *Both CH*

*Above* Although there is an 'old engineman's tale' of a Bulleid 'Pacific' reaching Portland during the Second World War, the story has never been substantiated. However, in 2003 a Bulleid 'Pacific' actually made it to the top of the Island at Easton, albeit on a low-loader. Brian Jackson photographed 'Merchant Navy' No 35018 *British India Line* awaiting restoration in a yard at Easton, Portland, on Thursday 8 April 2004. *British India Line* had hauled the first post-war 'Bournemouth Belle', and was also the first of the Bulleid 'Pacifics' to be rebuilt in 1956 (see also page 101). After withdrawal in 1964 she remained at Dai Woodham's yard at Barry, South Wales, until March 1980, when she was moved to the Mid Hants Railway. *Brian Jackson*

*Below* The Portland branch closed to passengers in March 1952, but until the late 1950s the first station on the branch, Melcombe Regis, was used on Summer Saturdays as an additional platform, being located adjacent to the main Weymouth station. An unidentified Bulleid 'Pacific' is seen at Melcombe Regis station on such a working, pulled up just short of the viaduct over Weymouth Backwater (now politely called Radipole Lake). This photograph illustrates the furthest south a Bulleid 'Pacific' locomotive is *known* to have worked. *The late J. D. Blackburn Collection*

These photographs do not show a Bulleid 'Pacific' locomotive, but merit inclusion in this book because of the historic significance of the event they illustrate. On Wednesday 9 July 2003 a ten-coach train, hauled by BR Standard Class 5 No 73096, made the round trip from Poole to Waterloo. No 73096 was built at the BR Derby Works in 1955, and was withdrawn from service only 12 years later. On the special train a champagne brunch was served on the up journey and a four-course dinner on the down, a good time being had by all. Some delay was experienced on the return journey, and it was clear that other trains on the line were disrupted. During a stop for water at Brockenhurst, ordinary fare-paying passengers were directed to catch the steam train, which then acted as a normal service train, making extra stops at New Milton and Christchurch. Thus passengers paying ordinary fares were conveyed by steam train – exactly 36 years to the day since the last time that had happened on this line! The upper photograph shows No 73096 during a water stop at Eastleigh on the outward journey, while the lower view shows the down run after arrival at Poole, after deputising as a service train from Brockenhurst onwards. *Both CH*

Saturday 6 December 2003 dawned raw and dull, but nothing could dampen the excitement of those lucky enough to travel on the first steam train to start from Wareham station for Waterloo since July 1967. I say lucky advisedly, because many more people had applied for tickets than there were seats available on the train, so I counted myself especially fortunate to secure a place in one of the dining carriages. The train was hauled throughout in both directions by 'Battle of Britain' Class No 34067 *Tangmere*, built as 21C167 in September 1947, renumbered 34067 in 1949 and withdrawn from BR service in November 1963.

The raw atmosphere of the December morning is captured in the top photograph showing *Tangmere* wreathed in steam and smoke at Wareham station. The train consisted of ten coaches of BR Standard Mark 2 stock, painted in a chocolate and cream livery. Hauling this load without assistance, *Tangmere* crested Parkstone bank with speed falling no lower than 34mph. A stop for water at Southampton Central gave the opportunity to take the centre photograph; *Tangmere* certainly looks more aesthetically pleasing than 4VEP unit No 3409 on the left. A fine run onwards to Waterloo followed, not spoiled in the least by being diverted via Staines and Feltham. The lower photograph shows *Tangmere* after arrival at Waterloo, surrounded by admiring passengers.

Despite leaving Waterloo 20 minutes late at 6.20pm, the return journey was of similarly high quality; notwithstanding a 10-minute stop for water at Hook, excellent locomotive performance saw the train arrive back at Wareham at 8.40pm. Even the carriage lights failing near Basingstoke, just as we were tucking into guinea fowl, if anything added to the trip – it made it possible to appreciate the white steam against the dark winter sky! How gratifying that even in the 21st century it is still possible to travel

behind a Bulleid 'Pacific' locomotive on the Waterloo to Weymouth line. *All CH*

# INDEX

**General**

'Bournemouth Belle' 14, 86, 101ff

Bulleid coaches 8, 19, 24, 28, 29, 35, 37, 39, 54, 60, 62, 67, 82, 83, 87, 88, 94, 123

Bulleid electric units 15, 30, 102

'The Royal Wessex' 19, 39, 40, 98

**Locations**

Alton 113, 120

Basingstoke 53-54

Bincombe Tunnel 5

Bluebell Railway 119, 123

Boscombe 69

Bournemouth Central 70-78
  loco depot 79-81
  West 2, 8, 64, 82-85, 106-110

Clapham Junction 35, 36, 103

Dorchester 91

Earlsfield 37, 38

Eastleigh 55-57, 126
  Works 13

Easton 125

Egham 114

Farlington Junction 116

Farnborough 48-52

Gas Works Junction, Branksome 106

Guildford 115

Holmsley 118

Melcombe Regis 125

National Railway Museum 12

New Malden 39, 40

Nine Elms loco depot 13

Parkstone 86

Poole 63, 87, 126

Portsmouth & Southsea 117

Raynes Park 39, 40

Ringwood 118

Ropley 120

Southampton Central 60-62, 65-68, 104-105, 127
  New Docks 68
  Ocean Terminal 59
  Old Docks 58-59
  Terminus 32, 58

Surbiton 41

Swanage 90, 124

Upwey & Broadwey 92

Vauxhall 34

Wareham 88, 127

Waterloo 14, 15-31, 101-103, 121, 127

Weymouth 14, 93, 94, 97-100, 122
  loco shed 93, 95-96

Wimbledon 39

Woking 42-47, 121

Worgret Junction 89

**Locomotives**
**'Merchant Navy' Class**

35001 8, 77, 92

35002 2

35003 14, 78, 105

35005 104, 122

35007 22, 27, 38

35008 49, 65, 76, 102, 103

35010 79

35011 22, 108

35012 97

35013 26, 47, 95, 114

35014 43, 106

35016 54, 96

35017 17, 57, 61

35018 101, 125

35019 39

35020 81

35021 17, 18, 19, 37

35023 35, 38

35024 18, 69

35025 70

35026 23, 109

35027 37, 60, 71

35028 40, 49, 55

35029 12, 107

35030 21, 46

**'West Country'/**
**'Battle of Britain' Class**

34001 92

34005 13, 72

34006 83, 91, 118

34008 72

34009 20, 41, 113

34010 14

34012 79

34016 75, 120

34017 60

34018 58

34020 5

34021 31, 74

34023 90, 100, 119

34024 29, 52

34025 30

34027 121

34028 124

34031 95

34033 59

34034 27

34036 69

34037 106, 110

34038 62, 115-116

34040 42, 48, 55

34043 19

34044 24

34046 50, 51, 84, 93

34047 52

34048 93, 96

34051 115

34057 82

34060 45, 94, 118

34061 86

34064 56

34066 36

34067 127

34071 34

34072 124

34076 56

34079 85

34084 74

34086 99

34087 33, 44, 66-67

34088 48, 53, 83, 114

34090 73

34091 98

34092 121

34093 25, 35, 41, 58

34094 80

34095 82

34097 59

34098 44

34100 27, 39

34102 51, 53, 54, 68, 87

34103 23

34104 28, 80

34105 120

34106 89

34110 88, 98